RE-FORMING THE PAST

RE-FORMING THE PAST

HISTORY, THE FANTASTIC, AND
THE POSTMODERN SLAVE NARRATIVE

A. TIMOTHY SPAULDING

THE OHIO STATE UNIVERSITY PRESS
Columbus

Library of Congress Cataloging-in-Publication Data
   Spaulding, A. Timothy.
   Re-forming the past : history, the fantastic, and the postmodern slave narrative /
   A. Timothy Spaulding.
       p. cm.
   Includes bibliographical references and index.
ISBN 0–8142–1006–6 (cloth : alk. paper)—ISBN 0–8142–9084–1 (CD-ROM)
1. American fiction—20th century—History and criticism. 2. Slavery in literature. 3.
American fiction—African American authors—History and criticism. 4. Johnson, Charles
Richard, 1948—Knowledge—History. 5. Historical fiction, American—History and criti-
cism. 6. Fantasy fiction, American—History and criticism. 7. Postmodernism (Literature)—
United States. 8. Reed, Ishmael, 1938– Flight to Canada. 9. African Americans in literature.
10. Butler, Octavia E. Kindred. 11. Morrison, Toni. Beloved. 12. Slaves in literature. I. Title.

PS374.S58S66 2005
813.'54093552—dc22
                2005003203

Cover design by Dan O'Dair.
Text design and typesetting by Jennifer Shoffey Forsythe.
Type set in Adobe Minion.
Printed by Thomson-Shore, Inc.

9 8 7 6 5 4 3 2

to the memory of

SHIRLEY BARBARA ATWELL,
YOU ARE STILL MY FIRST, LAST,
AND BEST AUDIENCE.

contents

acknowledgments

A LTHOUGH writing this book involved many hours writing in solitude in cramped spaces, I owe much of its content and completion to a number of individuals who influenced and supported me in a variety of ways.

James W. Coleman, Professor of African American Literature at the University of North Carolina, provided guidance and mentorship from the earliest stages of the project. His influence led me to place theory and African American literature in constant dialogue. Professor J. Lee Greene's insights, often rendered in lengthy late afternoon discussions, have also shaped my view of the relationship between critic and text. Both of these scholars have taught me in ways that will continue to inform my work.

The scholars whom I worked with at the University of North Carolina, Chapel Hill also played an instrumental role in the beginning stages of the project. Hilary Wyss, Erin Lang Bonin, Sandy Beardsley, Jennifer Halloran, Scott Walker, and Rick Incorvati all read numerous drafts and offered critical analyses that helped refine the project. The wide-ranging interests of all of these individuals compelled me to shape the project in interesting ways, always with a mind to clarify my arguments. Our commitment to one another as developing scholars is something I will always treasure.

My colleagues at the University of Delaware played an important role in encouraging me to push this project in new and often surprising directions. Alvina Quintana; her partner, Edward Guerrero; and Carol Henderson Belton provided support and encouragement, particularly when I needed it most: those moments of frustration when the words fail to do justice to the ideas behind them. My conversations about the writing process with Peter Feng also helped me to outlast those frustrations. The General University Research Grant from the University of Delaware provided much needed research support without which the completion of this project would have been difficult.

Miranda Wilson, my partner and friend, was instrumental in helping me reshape the project in ways that excited me and reinvigorated the writing process. The best ideas often happen at the oddest hours and must be worked through in conversation. Her willingness to do this was invaluable.

I believe it should never go without acknowledging the influence family has on one's work whether that influence is easily discernible or not. My sister, Pamela Spaulding, and my mother, Shirley Barbara Atwell, who passed away several years ago, are a part of everything I do. Locating their presence in my work is what allows me to keep writing.

The Slave Narrative and
Its Postmodern Counterpart

HE slave experience—a hallmark of physical, intellectual, and spiritual perseverance as much as a testament to America's betrayal of its
own democratic ideals—has always inspired African American writers. Slavery resonates in the entire oeuvre of African American literature,
leaving its trace most obviously in the original slave narratives and early
novels by African Americans such as William Wells Brown's *Clotel* (1853),
Frederick Douglass's 1845 *Narrative* and early novel *The Heroic Slave*
(1853), the recently discovered *Bondswoman's Narrative* (1855–1859), and
Harriet Wilson's *Our Nig* (1859) but also in the work of twentieth-century writers like Arna Bontemps (*Black Thunder,* 1936) and Margaret Walker
(*Jubilee,* 1966). Even more recent writers like Lorene Cary (*The Price of the
Child,* 1995) and Lalita Tademy (*Cane River,* 2000) continue to recall,
recast, and reinvent the slave experience, compelling us to examine the
heroic, tragic, and disturbing dimensions of American history. Narratives
of slavery constitute their own genre within African American literature—
one that reflects on not only the history of slavery but also its persistent
legacy in the present.

Within this genre, the texts that interest me most in *Re-Forming the
Past* are those that reject the boundaries of narrative realism in their
retelling of slavery. As a part of a larger tradition that sets out to recover
the stories of our past obscured by time and by an official historical record
that devalued the perspectives of the slaves themselves, many African
American writers, particularly in the last decades of the twentieth century,

sought not only to recover these stories, but also to redefine the way we narrate the slave experience. Writers such as Ishmael Reed, Octavia Butler, Toni Morrison, Charles Johnson, Samuel Delany, and Jewelle Gomez set out to correct the limited historical record on slavery and to critique traditional history's reliance on objectivity, authenticity, and realism as a means of representing the past. In their revisions of the slave narrative, these contemporary writers create an alternative and fictional historiography based on a subjective, fantastic, and anti-realistic representation of slavery. By rejecting realism as both a narrative mode and a literary genre, these writers do more than question the nature of historical representation. They use the fantastic and genres like science fiction, the gothic novel, postmodern metafiction, and the vampire tale to claim authority over the history of slavery and the historical record. When the ghost makes her appearance in physical form in Toni Morrison's *Beloved,* when Ishmael Reed's slave protagonist boasts of his escape from slavery in an airplane in *Flight to Canada,* when the narrator of *Oxherding Tale* interrupts his story and forces us to question the very nature of first-person narration, when an unnamed slave girl is transformed into an ageless vampire in *The Gilda Stories,* these texts decidedly embrace a non-mimetic approach to slavery and pose challenging interpretive dilemmas for us as readers.

The primary questions I address in this book are: What theoretical foundations lay at the heart of this non-mimetic approach to history? What do formal devices and literary genres generally regarded as unrealistic offer these African American writers in their accounts of slavery? How do we or, perhaps, should we even locate authority, authenticity, and verisimilitude (or in more direct, albeit elusive terms: truth) in these texts when they draw on forms that undermine these concepts? A short answer would be this: the literary and aesthetic freedom accorded generic forms like the gothic novel or science fiction defamiliarize both the history of slavery and traditional approaches to writing that history. By deploying elements of the fantastic or metafiction in their texts, these writers force us to question the ideologies embedded within the "realistic" representation of slavery in traditional history and historical fiction. In its place, Reed, Morrison, Butler, and others reconstruct an overtly oppositional, highly fictionalized form of history—one that allows them to claim authority over the narrative construction of past. As such, their revisions of slave narratives simultaneously politicize the non-mimetic devices and genres they use in their texts and aestheticize the act of writing history.

The contemporary African American writer's preoccupation with the ideological underpinnings of realism and its effects on the historical discourse on slavery constitutes an African American *postmodern* approach to the slave narrative. In his analysis of the rise of the neo-slave narrative form, Ashraf Rushdy argues that the neo-slave narrative bears the mark of the cultural politics of the late sixties, a period which "saw the emergence of world-historical political movements that created new social subjects [and] raise[d] anew questions about race and racial identity, literature and literary history, texts and intertextuality" (*Neo-slave* 7). Although Rushdy focuses primarily on the impact of black cultural nationalism on the historiography of slavery and, subsequently, on the rise of the neo-slave narratives of the seventies and eighties, I would argue that the discourse of postmodernism played as crucial a role in the development of the texts I examine in this study. All of the novels were written during the period of time most associated with the rise and development of postmodernism as a theoretical and cultural discourse. In addition, these texts share many of the key preoccupations of postmodern aesthetics and politics. In their critique of traditional history, the postmodern slave narrative engages in the dismantling of Enlightenment conceptions of history and identity and the totalizing grand narrative of Western cultural superiority. Spanning from Ishmael Reed's *Flight to Canada* (1976) to Jewelle Gomez's *The Gilda Stories* (1991), these novels engage, to varying degrees, aspects of postmodern subjectivity, history, and textuality by examining the instability of our narrative representation of the past. However, even as they reject realism and embrace non-mimetic devices in their treatment of history (a quality they share with other postmodern fictions), many writers of postmodern slave narratives retain a stable conception of identity and historical authority that comes out of the cultural and racial politics of the sixties and is, at times, at odds with postmodern thought. In so doing, these writers forge a distinctly African American form of postmodernism—one influenced by postmodern thought but rooted in black history and informed by black identity politics.[1]

The contemporary black writer's treatment of slavery reveals a tense relationship between the anti-foundationalism of postmodernism's stance on history and the black nationalist goal of reclaiming that past. Postmodernism as a discourse emphasizes the distinction between the real events of the past from our access to it through the discursive representation. As a result, the historical fiction normally associated with postmodernism, texts like Thomas Pynchon's *Gravity's Rainbow* or Salman Rushdie's *Midnight's Children,* bracket the past from their representation of it through parody and pastiche.[2] Most postmodern slave narratives reject the parodic aspects of the postmodern treatment of history (with the notable exceptions of Ishmael Reed and Charles Johnson) and opt for a more serious approach even as they displace realism as the primary narrative mode of history. Rather than emphasizing the discursive representation of slavery over its historical realities or undermining the stability or agency of the individual subject, many of these texts reinvest narrative historical representation with a determinacy and agency that harkens back to the original slave narratives. What results in these novels is a persistent faith in the power and ability of narrative (if used oppositionally) to achieve liberation for both the enslaved and the postmodern black subject.

Writers of postmodern slave narratives view the history of slavery as in need of *re-formation*. In sociopolitical terms, these writers set out to re-form our conception of American slavery by depicting a more complex, nuanced view of black identity in the context of American slavery. In aesthetic terms, they seek to create a new narrative form through which to reveal the complexities embedded within the slave experience and obscured by traditional historical accounts. They begin by expanding the parameters of narrative and historical realism that constructed and, in some ways, perpetuated the dehumanizing effects of slavery under the guise of objectivity. Like its eighteenth- and nineteenth-century counterpart, the postmodern slave narrative represents a political act of narration designed to reshape our view of slavery and its impact on our cultural condition. It is designed to intrude upon history as a means to re-form it. Unlike the original slave narratives, however, these texts define themselves by their ability to stretch the formal conventions of traditional history and the original slave narratives themselves. They call attention to their own process of re-forming slavery, not merely as a metafictional enterprise but also as a way of revitalizing the historiography of slavery. Rather than drawing on elements of the sentimental novel and nineteenth-century spiritual autobiographies as the original slave narratives did, postmodern slave narratives draw from nonrealistic genres in order to re-form our view of the past. By infusing more contemporary genres like science fiction and the postmodern novel or even older forms like the gothic (which, arguably, has retained its popularity in newer guises) into their narratives, these writers appeal to contemporary readers much as nineteenth-century writers mined genres familiar to their readers. The narrative freedom these popular genres offer contemporary writers also allow them to dismantle the conventionalized representation of slavery that constrains our understanding of this vital dimension of our national past.

Although American slavery and its legacy are common tropes in many contemporary novels, I make a distinction between those texts that fall under the general classifications of "neo-slave narratives" and those that demonstrate a particular orientation toward fictional and historical representation. Generally, the term "neo-slave narrative" refers to contemporary texts that deal with slavery in its historical context (texts like Sherley Anne Williams's *Dessa Rose* or Morrison's *Beloved*), through its resonance in our contemporary moment (texts like David Bradley's *The Chaneysville Incident* or Gayl Jones's *Corrigedora*), or through a reinvention of the formal characteristics of the original slave narratives (texts like Ishmael Reed's *Flight to Canada* or Charles Johnson's *Oxherding Tale*).[3] The novels I discuss exhibit all of the general aspects of neo-slave narratives. However, what links novels like *Flight to Canada* and Johnson's *Middle Passage,* or even Toni Morrison's *Beloved* and Octavia Butler's *Kindred,* are the ways these novels rely on non-mimetic genres and devices in order to claim historical authority in their depiction of American slavery. Rather than focusing on the historical context of slavery or examining its legacy, these texts use elements of the fantastic to occupy the past, the present, and, in some cases, the future simultaneously. Rather than merely imitating or revising the slave narrative form, the postmodern slave narrative critiques historical and fictional representations that rely on claims of verisimilitude. These novels call into question our tendency to regard realism as the ideal narrative mode for history and historical fiction; they implicitly assert that claims of authenticity, realism, and objectivity result, particularly in the discourse on slavery, in a potentially oppressive obfuscation of the past.

Perhaps the clearest way to distinguish the orientation of history in the postmodern slave narrative from more traditional fictional treatments of slavery, even those written by other African Americans, is to compare the narrative project underlying Toni Morrison's *Beloved* and the one underlying Barbara Chase-Riboud's 1979 novel, *Sally Hemmings*. Although both texts return to the history of slavery, each exhibits a distinct perspective on the act of writing and reclaiming history. Chase-Riboud focuses her historical fiction on the enslaved black mistress of Thomas Jefferson and asserts that her primary inspiration for the novel was the desire to tell the story of a real woman obscured by the official historical record. While Chase-Riboud acknowledges the fact that many historians intentionally conspired to keep Sally Hemmings's story hidden, she maintains a basic faith in the traditional historical process. In an "Author's Note" to the 1994 edition of the novel, Chase-Riboud writes:

> [I]n a free nation, History should be revered, not the people who make or
> write it. And this history should be revered, warts and all, with all the

dangerous passions, secrets, contradictions, anachronistic interpretations, dark undersides, and self-preserving lies that go with the mythology of a nation, and should be revised often.

For history is nothing more than the human adventure as told by fallible humans, with all their prejudices and psychoses and visions, to the society, which they serve. The result is sometimes, even most often, "scientific" truth, but not always. (354)

Barbara Chase-Riboud questions the motivations behind those who have written the histories of American slavery and points out the ideological concerns that shape the ways they have reconstructed the past. In attempting to shed light on Thomas Jefferson's affair with Sally Hemmings, she met with severe opposition from historians she calls "Jeffersonians," who took offense at the ramifications this affair would have on his historical character. She makes the distinction, however, between the Jeffersonians who attempt to obscure "blemishes" of the past and what she calls History. Some historians, she argues, taint what is most often a "scientific" project. She frames her own fictional representation of the past as a return to the fundamental truth intrinsic to the traditional historical project. The novel, in essence, seeks to correct the historical record by adding this particular aspect of Jefferson's (and Hemmings's) past. This addition complicates the mythology surrounding this complex and revered figure by revealing the mythology's "dark underside." Rather than deconstructing the foundation of traditional Western historiography, Chase-Riboud retains a faith in the historical process and its ability to reflect truth. Though she clearly employs the imaginative characteristics of the sentimental romance as a means to illuminate her story, the novel contains no explicit abandonment of realistic conventions or critique of the historical process. More closely resembling Margaret Mitchell's *Gone with the Wind* in its form and content as a historical romance, *Sally Hemmings*'s main contribution to the representation of slavery is its depiction of a story untold.

Postmodern slave narratives like *Beloved* question not only the ideologies hidden within specific historical representations of slavery but also those ideologies that form the basis of Western historiography. Like Chase-Riboud, Toni Morrison bases her novel on a real historical figure. In Morrison's case she turns to Margaret Garner, a slave woman convicted of murdering one of her four children in an attempt to free the child from enslavement. In contrast to Chase-Riboud's fictional reconstruction of the past, Morrison's narrative eschews realism, objectivity, and linearity and calls attention to the inadequacy of traditional historiography, particularly in its treatment of American slavery. In its place, Morrison provides readers with a narrative form that draws on memory, oral culture, and elements of the fantastic as structural and thematic devices. Morrison establishes Beloved as both a ghost figure in the gothic tradition and a symbolic metaphor that stands in for all those lives lost as a result of slavery and the middle passage. This construction allows her to explore the spiritual and psychological dimensions of those who endured slavery even as she undermines (or at least complicates) the verisimilitude of her text. In spite of this infusion of the fantastic, Morrison suggests that the fictional text, with its dialogic quality and its emphasis on imagination, can succeed where traditional historiography and historical fiction fail.[4]

In spite of my classification of the postmodern slave narrative under one conceptual framework, it is important to acknowledge the diverse ways these texts and their authors re-form the history of slavery. Far from adhering to a singular of common ideological stance, the writers I discuss (Ishmael Reed, Octavia Butler, Toni Morrison, Charles Johnson, Jewelle Gomez, and Samuel Delany) each posit a re-formation of the past that comments on the postmodern condition of black subjectivity in unique ways. In many ways, Reed and Johnson create texts that most retain the parodic and metafictional aspects of white postmodernist texts. As a result, their novels undermine traditional or romanticized conceptions of a stable or autonomous black subject. The novels by Butler, Morrison, and Gomez emphasize the links between black women across time and space. As such, these writers reject, or at least critique, the postmodern view of the subject. Where Gomez and Delaney create texts that project slavery into the future as a means of re-forming the past, Morrison and Butler emphasize the ways the past history of slavery intrudes upon the present with disturbing and dangerous consequences. And although most postmodern slave narratives turn to other fantastic or non-mimetic forms to re-form the history and historiography of slavery, Charles Johnson's texts turn inward to the slave narrative form as a means of re-forming the past.

Ultimately, what sets the postmodern slave narrative apart is its orientation toward the act of representing slavery in narrative form. By creating characters that defy the conventions of time and space (as both Butler and Reed do), by using formal devices that subvert the conventions of narrative realism (as Morrison and Johnson do), or by mining genres that many regard as escapist (as Delany and Gomez do), African American writers re-form traditional historical representations of slavery from a contemporary perspective. They compel us to re-examine the past in a way that acknowledges its impact on the present. Part of that process requires that we place the postmodern slave narrative in a historical context—one that examines its foundation in the original slave narratives of the eighteenth and nineteenth centuries.

Revisiting the Original Slave Narrative

The fact that African American writers have returned to the slave narrative so frequently almost 150 years since the abolition of slavery raises questions as to why that literary form continues to resonate in our contemporary moment. As Hazel Carby points out, while slavery has always been central to the African American literary imagination, until recently slavery has rarely been "the focus of the imaginative physical and geographical terrain of the Afro-American novel" (125). Carby offers three explanations for African American writers' frequent return to the slave narrative. First, the slave narrative represents the framework of the African American literary tradition and thus perpetuates a sustained interest in the historical context of that tradition. Second, Carby suggests that the material and physical conditions of slavery represent a "prehistory" that can explain contemporary phenomena. Third, Carby suggests that the "ideology of the folk" which dominates African American fiction has its roots in the slave experience.[5] The original eighteenth- and nineteenth-century slave narratives represent our most direct account of this crucial component of American history and our most immediate access to the identities of those who fought so desperately for freedom. In returning to this historical moment, contemporary writers remind us of our past and pay tribute to those who successfully navigated the cultural terrain that sought to enslave them. However, for all the information the original or traditional slave narratives provide us on the conditions of slavery, these texts often veiled the most disturbing aspects of slavery in order to appeal to a primarily white audience. As a result, the contemporary writer's relationship to the original slave narratives is complex, evoking both vexation at the forces which constrained the form and admiration for the ways the writers were able to negotiate those constraints.

For writers of the postmodern slave narrative, simply recovering the voices of those who endured slavery is not enough. They set out to re-form the slave narrative itself, as a document and critique of American slavery, by recovering the ideological project that served as the slave narrative's original foundation. The original slave narratives, most of which were written by men and women who gained their freedom and their knowledge of written English under the most degrading and dehumanizing of circumstances, provide the contemporary writer with a useful model for textual production. More than a simple description of the flight from slavery to freedom, the traditional slave narratives, as a form of autobiography, offer a narrative representation of black identity itself; they provide a discursive model of black subjectivity in narrative performance. In his study of early African American autobiography, William Andrews argues that the slave narrative, in its declaration of an empowered and free self, involves a "psycholiterary quest." This quest represents a crucial process in which the author

> *declares* himself through various linguistic acts . . . [which] include the reconstructing of one's past in a meaningful and instructive form, the appropriating of empowering myths and models of the self from any available resources, and the redefining of one's place in the scheme of things by redefining the language used to locate one in that scheme. (7)

In keeping with this definition, contemporary writers draw on these same linguistic acts when they revisit narratives by escaped slaves. But in its contemporary re-formation, it is slavery itself that provides these writers with a past in need of reconstruction, the escaped slave who represents the empowering model of selfhood, and the language of the slave narrative as a text that contemporary writers redefine in order to locate themselves in the overall discourse on slavery and its legacy.

As much as the foundation of the traditional slave narrative relies on the former slave's declaration of a free self, these texts resist locating that conception of self in romanticized notions of American freedom and identity. The slave narrative is both an expression of emergent sense of selfhood and a moral indictment of an American culture that has systematically oppressed that self. While the slave narrative reveres notions of democratic freedom and identity, it also contextualizes these concepts by juxtaposing them with images of slavery. A free identity in the slave narrative is one wrought with the physical and mental abuses of enslavement, the cultural and familial alienation of being stripped from one's homeland and family, and the internal traumas of being treated as a subhuman commodity. And, in many instances, the slave narrators point out that theirs is, at best, a contested freedom. In perhaps the most widely read slave narrative, *Narrative of the Life of Frederick Douglass,* Douglass stresses the fact that, even after he has achieved freedom in the North, he must live with the constant threat of being recaptured and the prejudice against his race, both of which make it difficult for him to find employment. The North represents freedom for Douglass and other escaped slaves. However, it is a safe haven in only the most limited sense—one where racism and the threat of re-enslavement still exist. For the slave narrator, the notion of a free identity involves both an internal and external dynamic, each entwined with the other. Even when he or she gains the internal sense of a free identity, the external world operates in opposition to that self, making freedom always a deferred and conditional concept.

In returning to the slave narrative form, contemporary writers similarly critique idealized notions of freedom and identity. From a contemporary vantage point, one still marked by racial tensions, continuing economic and social inequities, and persistent notions of racial superiority, writers who revisit slavery and its discursive forms draw explicit and implicit connections between the escaped slave's limited sense of freedom and the hardships facing contemporary African Americans. For the contemporary writer, true freedom from systematized and individual expressions of racism remains deferred. Consequently, writers must continually critique commodity culture and scrutinize the ways the legacies of slavery work to constrain African Americans' sense of self. Ultimately, the slave narrative and its postmodern counterpart produce a critique of American culture as much as an expression of African American subjectivity; the underlying project is cultural critique wrapped up in the expression of identity.

The slave narrative also represents the foundation of the African American literary tradition in general and the African American novel more specifically. Marked by a first-person account of the slave's life and a bipartite structure of the movement from (Southern) slavery to (Northern) freedom, the slave narrative was the creative form of choice for many African American writers who sought to recreate their experience for a wide audience. As a form of popular literature, the original slave narratives drew on standard conventions that linked it to several other fictional generic forms of the day such as the sentimental novel (through its melodramatic descriptions of escapes), the picaresque novel (through its episodic structure and the slave narrator's resemblance to the picaro), and the conversion narrative (with its religious overtones of the "ascension" from slavery to freedom). Henry Louis Gates Jr. argues that the slave narrative itself "is a countergenre, a mediation between the novel of sentiment and the picaresque, oscillating between the two in a bipolar moment, set in motion by the mode of confession" (81). This narrative strategy provided the basic structure for nineteenth-century African American novels such as Frank Webb's *The Garies and Their Friends* (1857) and Frances Harper's *Iola Leroy* (1892).[6] In revisiting the slave narrative, African American writers consciously return to the roots of the African American novel tradition and reflect on its impact on their own work. The postmodern slave narrative's deployment of multiple genres and conventions like time and space travel, and ghosts and vampires, recalls the original slave narratives' status as a countergenre. As such, the "postmodern" dimensions of these novels owe as much, if not more, to the influence of their eighteenth- and nineteenth-century counterparts as they do to the influence of the theoretical discourse of postmodernism.

Even in the original slave narratives, the presence of fictional devices served a rhetorical function designed to engage a wider readership through its connection with popular sensibilities of the time. Frances Foster, in *Witnessing Slavery,* argues that, although the slave narrative appealed to nineteenth-century readers' appetites for the sensationalism of sentimental novels by depicting the dangers of escaping slavery, these elements were not "concocted to appeal only to the heightened sensibilities of romantic females or any other mass audience" but worked in tandem with the narrator's desire to convert his readers (23). Although the incorporation of fictive elements in the original slave narratives does not prove that early African American writers consciously manipulated the popular demands of their white readers for their own political ends, it does suggest that their narratives successfully negotiated the limitations of a white readership that seemed to prefer sentimentalized depictions of slavery. The postmodern slave narrative's use of fantastic elements, then, finds a precursor in the original slave narratives. Rather than manipulating the conventions of the sentimental novel, however, postmodern slave narratives mine the conventions of science fiction, fantasy, and the postmodern novel to appeal to contemporary sensibilities.

Ultimately, the slave narrative provides the contemporary writer with a complex model of narrative hybridity. Even in the most basic terms, the form represents the intersection between creative and autobiographical expression, between historical and fictional representation, between the individual quest for freedom and the larger political goals of cultural critique. Stephen Butterfield, in his study of black autobiography, points out that the slave narrator's status as a former slave, as a member of the movement to abolish slavery, and as a free person suffering racial discrimination in the North necessitated a hybrid approach to narrating his or her life— one which merged the autobiographical act with historical and political discourse. In essence, early African American authors became fiction writers, historians, and political polemicists even as they told their own life stories. As a result, "they feel free to range over the whole subject of race relations and anti-slavery politics. Their personal careers merge so closely with the political movement that relating the story of their lives is a political act" (28). In this merger of autobiography, history, and political discourse, the slave narrative works as a multi-layered rhetorical strategy even as it exists as a document of personal identity.

The slave narrative's tendency to slide between multiple discourses simultaneously offers an obvious appeal to the contemporary writer. The slave narrative, in essence, prefigures the postmodern preoccupation with pastiche and discursive multiplicity. And yet, unlike some postmodern texts that deploy multiple literary and cultural forms in a display of literary virtuosity, parody, and narrative play, the slave narrative's hybrid form comes out of a clear and directed discursive strategy—one designed to affect a specific political situation and historical condition. As a prototype for its postmodern counterpart, the slave narrative represents an early model of postmodern discourse—one that combines multiple narrative forms and rhetorical strategies to produce a hybrid of personal expression, popular elements, and politically motivated cultural critique. By retaining an explicit connection to the original slave narratives, writers of the postmodern slave narrative retain an agency and a faith in the power of narrative that implicitly critique and ultimately transform the discourse of postmodernism.

African American Postmodernism: Black Nationalism, Black Feminism, and Postmodern Theory in Contested Conversation

It is important to note that my use of the term "postmodernism" in defining this genre within contemporary African American fiction refers to only one discourse at work in these contemporary examinations of slavery. In fact, the orientation toward slavery at work in these texts actually arose from a nexus of discourses, all of which confront the nature of historical representation, individual and cultural identity, and the impact of Eurocentrism and commodity culture in the late twentieth century. Specifically, as I have argued, postmodern slave narratives arose from the complicated interaction between black cultural nationalism, black feminism, and postmodernism. Each of these discourses posited alternative and complex conceptions of history, identity, and political agency which found their way into these texts in often conflicting and conflicted ways. The postmodern slave narrative's rejection of narrative realism in its approach to history—a project that was particularly prevalent in the 1970s and 1980s—illuminates the contested conversation between these discourses and provides a way to examine their complicated interaction. My decision to refer to these texts as "postmodern" results less from a sense that postmodernism is the dominant discourse at work in these texts and more from the fact that they arose during a period most literary and cultural critics refer to as the postmodern.

Theories of the postmodern began to proliferate in the academy in the late sixties and early seventies, arising, in part, out of a desire to distinguish between high-modernist cultural production of the early twentieth century and the cultural formations of the latter half of the century.[7] Abandoning the Cartesian faith in a unified and coherent individual derived from a universal human essence, European and Euro-American postmodern theorists posited that the individual subject was a culturally overdetermined product of ideological forces that pre-existed and defined it. This shift represented a profound decentering of the individual consciousness in contemporary thought. In addition, postmodernism called into question claims of absolute or objective truth characteristic of Enlightenment thinking, emphasizing the subjectivity and contingency of all truth claims. Postmodernism as a discourse placed in flux all faith in traditional conceptions of identity, aesthetic or cultural value, and history. Postmodernism also theorizes the effects late capitalism, consumer culture, and advances in science and technology have had on the late twentieth and early twenty-first centuries. As such, it offers a potentially useful critical framework through which to examine the lives of contemporary African Americans.

In spite of opening critical spaces in which to interrogate the hegemony of Western culture, most early conceptions of postmodernism offered no commentary on the specific experiences of African Americans. Many postmodernist theorists and critics perpetuated this hegemony by referring primarily (and often exclusively) to white cultural forms in their critical analyses. As James Coleman argues in *Black Male Fiction and the Legacy of Caliban,* because "black writers do not start from a position of equality . . . [the] liberating potential [of postmodernism] is not the same as it is for white writers" (5). As a result, "they must generate the voice to construct liberating fictions *against* the hegemony of Western discourse" (5) of which "postmodernism" is very much a part. Black writers of the postmodern slave narratives construct this voice and create these fictions by incorporating aspects of black nationalism and black feminism into their treatments of history, thus altering the conceptual foundations of postmodernism itself.[8] These competing discourses form the basis of an overtly ideological and distinctly African American form of postmodernism.

African American postmodernism conceptualizes the nature of fragmented subjectivity and cultural identity in distinct and often oppositional ways from its white counterpart because of the residual influence of black nationalism. Black nationalism arose in the late sixties and early seventies as a response not only to a long history of white racism but also to the limited success of the civil rights movement in achieving equal opportunities for African Americans. As exemplified by the Black Power and Black Arts movements, black nationalism involved a combination of aesthetic theory and political praxis that marked a shift from an integrationist stance toward white America to an Afrocentric view of black culture. Political activists like Stokely Carmichael and Willie Ricks called for a revolutionary stance against the economic and political dominance of capitalism and white America. Cultural theorists like LeRoi Jones, Stephen Henderson, and Addison Gayle theorized the foundations of a distinct and unified black aesthetic in opposition to the hegemony of white mainstream culture. In both instances, black nationalists perpetuated the existence of an essentialist view of black identity in their celebration of the strength and cohesiveness of black culture and black consciousness.[9]

In the context of Enlightenment thought, conceptions of a rich black cultural heritage and black consciousness deconstructed notions of white supremacy while upholding the traditional conceptions of individual autonomy, the stability of racial identity, and the possibility of historical authenticity. For black nationalists struggling to achieve political and cultural gains within the stultifying constraints of white America, the postmodernist deconstruction of individual identity, cultural cohesion, and objective truth claims posed almost as great a challenge to black activism as Eurocentrism had. Black nationalists responded to the double threat of Eurocentrism and postmodernism by constructing a limited and, in many ways, masculinist conception of black identity.

The rise of black feminist theory and criticism in the seventies was, in part, a response by black women to their limited presence in the discourse of black nationalism.[10] Although major figures such as Sonya Sanchez, Carolyn Rodgers, Angela Davis, and others participated in the Black Arts and Black Power movements, black nationalism of the late sixties and early seventies remained a largely masculinist movement fueled by the concerns of black male identity. Early black feminist literary critics like Alice Walker, Audre Lorde, and Barbara Christian sought to recover the literary tradition of black women writers that black nationalism had ignored. More recent feminist critics like bell hooks often critique the patriarchal dimensions of black nationalism, arguing that any view of black identity must examine the interaction of race, class, gender, and sexuality. More than merely adding gender to the discourse of black nationalism, the development of black feminist theory and criticism in the early seventies and eighties complicated and deepened conceptions of black identity. However, even in the context of this transformation, black feminist critics retained a conception of identity that opposed postmodern theories of subjectivity. In fact, just as black nationalists emphasized the cohesiveness of black culture, many black feminists viewed the community of black women as a unified and spiritually empowering collective. Patricia Hill Collins, while acknowledging the benefits of postmodern theory in terms of its deconstruction of white, Western hegemony, argues that the political implications of postmodernism raise three particular concerns for Black feminist thought: 1) its inability to construct new explanations for social phenomena; 2) its rejection of all claims of credibility, legitimation, and authority; and 3) its tendency to undermine African American women's group authority (139–43). Black feminist theorists such as Collins and bell hooks argue that black women should not abandon all concepts of authority but should instead claim authority based on their complex and varied identities as black women.

Many contemporary black feminist critics emphasize African American women's lived experiences as the basis for their collective authority. Collins asserts that black women can achieve political and cultural mobilization only when they use their diverse experiences to create a collective identity:

> Individual African American women have long displayed varying types of consciousness regarding our shared angle of vision. By aggregating and articulating these individual expressions of consciousness, a collective group consciousness becomes possible. Black women's ability to forge these individual, unarticulated, yet potentially powerful expressions of everyday consciousness into an articulated, self-defined, collective standpoint is key to Black women's survival. (26)

Collins conceptualizes black women's collectivity as the product of both shared and individualized experiences. In the process of articulating these experiences, united by the *cultural context* of race, class, and gender oppression, black women achieve "a collective group consciousness." Similarly, bell hooks argues that black women's struggle for critical authority necessitates not only an emphasis on the cultural connections between them but also a rejection of essentialist notions of identity which may exclude the individual experiences of many African American women. For hooks, this exclusion undermines potentially liberating notions of selfhood that would offer diverse expressions of black subjectivity. In a time when views of what constitutes "blackness" are often radically diverse, any conception of black subjectivity must "affirm multiple black identities, varied black experience" that "opposes reinscribing notions of 'authentic' black identity" (28). However, hooks, like Collins, remains unwilling to reject all notions of authenticity:

> Part of our struggle for radical black subjectivity is the quest to find ways to construct self and identity that is oppositional and liberatory. The unwillingness to critique essentialism on the part of many African Americans is rooted in the fear that it will cause folks to lose sight of the specific history and experience of African-Americans and the unique sensibilities and culture that arise from that experience. An adequate response to this concern is to critique essentialism while emphasizing the significance of "the authority of experience." There is a radical difference between a repudiation of the idea that there is a black "essence" and recognition of the way black identity has been specifically constituted in the experience of exile and struggle. (29)

An "authority of experience" allows black women to claim identification with one another based not only on their racial and gendered identities but also on a shared political project. As a result, black feminist theory establishes a space where alternative conceptions of identity and collectivity allow them to claim a position of authority.

In *Signs and Cities: Black Literary Postmodernism*, Madhu Dubey argues that African Americans and the cultural texts they produce occupy a paradoxical space in postmodern discourse. On one level, many African Americans, along with other racial and ethnic minorities in the United States, "have suffered heavily from the material processes distinctive of the postmodern era" and, as such, are fundamentally a part of postmodern discourse (8). However, on another level, African Americans are also "fetishized as the guarantors of everything that is felt to be at risk in the postmodern era—bodily presence, palpable reality, political intentionality" (8). Dubey suggests that this paradox arises out of the tendency of postmodern cultural critics to synthesize aesthetic indeterminacy and racial essentialism—a form of having our cake and eating it too (10). Most writers of the postmodern slave narrative engage in this synthesis and thus occupy a paradoxical space both inside and outside postmodern discourse. However, rather than a limitation of their narratives, this paradox illustrates the tensions that arise, even in our contemporary moment, when black writers attempt to conceptualize a liberating identity and historiography from a minority position. These texts reflect the tenuous definitions of racial identity we not only struggle to dismantle but also struggle to account for.

Any conception of African American postmodernism must acknowledge the complex relationship between black nationalism, black feminist identity politics, and postmodern theory. While white theories of the postmodern undermine the hegemony of white mainstream culture from within, African American postmodernism attempts to dismantle it from a marginalized position. This approach has two implications at the level of cultural critique: 1) the positions of marginality and centrality must be destabilized, thus rendering them open and contested spaces, and 2) postmodernism itself must be reconceptualized to include the specific challenges of African American subjectivity in contemporary culture. Ultimately, African American postmodernism rejects marginalization and emphasizes black perspectives, acknowledging that, even when African Americans occupy a marginalized status in the context of mainstream American culture, they must occupy postmodern discourse from a more centralized position. African American postmodernism, then, provides us with both a critique and an extension of postmodernism.

From Indeterminacy to Authority:
History and Identity in the Postmodern Slave Narrative

As a product of African American postmodernism, the postmodern slave narrative's treatment of history and identity reflects the political ideology of black nationalism, the "authority of experience" and identity politics of black feminism, and the deconstructive project of postmodernism. From these discourses, African American writers develop a concept of "narrative authority" that reinvests the contemporary writer with political agency by radicalizing the act of storytelling. Rather than masking the subjective presence or the imaginative dimensions of their reconstructions of the past, writers such as Ishmael Reed and Toni Morrison emphasize the cultural, political, and ideological connections between themselves and the subjects of their texts. They infuse their texts with fantastic or non-mimetic devices to create a paradoxical narrative form. In essence, postmodern slave narratives deploy elements of the fantastic not as a way of undermining their narrative authority but as a means of establishing it. Through the narrative freedom of imaginative or speculative fiction, postmodern slave narratives blur the lines between historical subject and contemporary author, between the past history of slavery and its current legacy in contemporary culture, between historical and fictional reconstructions of the past.

In many ways, the postmodern slave narrative's treatment of History coincides with "traditional" or Eurocentric postmodernist fiction. Specifically, African American writers' rejection of realism and their reliance on non-mimetic elements resembles a similar stance undertaken by white postmodernist writers. In *Postmodernist Fiction* Brian McHale argues that postmodern historical fiction, as opposed to "classic" historical fiction, emphasizes the fictional text's opposition to the official record by creating an alternative and fantastic version of history in its place. As a result, these texts create what McHale calls an "ontological flicker between the two worlds: one moment, the official version seems to be eclipsed by the apocryphal version; the next moment, it is the apocryphal version that seems mirage-like" (90).[11] McHale argues that postmodern writers, in their suspicion of the hidden ideologies masked behind claims of truth, realism, or objectivity, focus on the inherently subjective and conditional aspects of all narrative representations of the past. As a result, neither the official historical record nor their own fictional reconstructions of history stand as adequate or accurate representations of the past. Readers are left with an undetermined space in the place of history. Similarly, Linda Hutcheon, in *A Poetics of Postmodernism,* argues that postmodernist fiction places itself in opposition to traditional history by refuting "common sense" methods of distinguishing between historical fact and fiction. Many postmodern texts take the form of what she calls "historiographic metafiction": narratives that, through the interaction between historiography and metafiction, reject claims of authentic representation, challenge artistic originality, and highlight the transparency of historical referentiality. In these instances, the subject under interrogation becomes the narrative method or text rather than the past events they seek to represent.

Implicit in both Hutcheon's and McHale's conception of postmodern historical fiction is the refusal of these texts to treat the past as a real event untainted by the effects of narrative representation. As a result, postmodern historical fiction fails to posit any viable narrative constructions of the past in place of the history which it would dispense. Fredric Jameson characterizes the postmodern aesthetic impulse as the attempt to historicize the present "in an age when we have forgotten how to think historically in the first place" (*Postmodernism* ix). This memory loss emerges from a "society bereft of all historicity . . . [in which] the past as 'referent' finds itself gradually bracketed, and then effaced altogether, leaving us with nothing but texts" (18). Terry Eagleton, in *The Illusions of Postmodernism,* similarly critiques the depthless postmodern gesture toward history. Eagleton argues that postmodernism, in its rejection of historical objectivity and continuity, limits postmodernism's ability to confront the past with any political efficacy.[12]

Many postmodern slave narratives avoid the historical indeterminacy that Jameson and Eagleton attribute to postmodernism primarily by retaining a concept of narrative authority rooted in a sense of communal identity As a result, for writers like Morrison and Butler, narrative reconstructions of the past can achieve authority and potentially liberating qualities on the basis of the communal connection between author, narrator, and historical subject. In a sense, the past history of slavery in these texts is real and present, subject to reinterpretation in direct and concrete ways. These narratives approach slavery not as an event isolated by time and space or abstracted by the narrative act, but rather as one of the continuing grand narratives of Western domination that links the contemporary author to the historical subject. As a result, many postmodern slave narratives claim to reconstruct a more complete view of the past from a present perspective—a view that the official history effaces and postmodernism abstracts. As we will see throughout many of these novels, the use of imaginative devices and themes, such as anachronism, time travel, "rememory," produce not McHale's "ontological flicker" but an authoritative and overtly political re-formation of the past. By erasing the boundaries of time and space, African American writers claim the authority to re-form history from their present perspective and compel readers to embrace an expansive, imaginative, and liberating representation of slavery. Historical theorist Hayden White, drawing on such postmodernist and post-structuralist writers as Michel Foucault and Paul Ricoeur, argues for a similar acknowledgment of imagination as a necessary or inevitable part of narrative history. In *The Content of the Form,* he writes:

[J]ust as the contents of myth are tested by fiction, so, too, the forms of fiction are tested by (narrative) historiography. If in a similar manner the content of narrative historiography is tested to determine its adequacy to represent and explain another order of reality than that presupposed by traditional historians, this should be seen less as an opposition of science to ideology . . . than as a continuation of the process of mapping the limit between the imaginary and the real which begins with the invention of fiction itself. (45)

Deconstructing the relationship between "science" and "history," White places narrative history on the same continuum with "myth" and "fiction." Rather than purely oppositional constructs, myth, history, and fiction are relational, sharing similar aspects of the imaginary and the real. Writers of the postmodern slave narrative draw from all of these elements in order to construct their fictional histories—their historical fictions.[13]

Although postmodern slave narratives reject traditional conceptions of history, many also reject the self-referential preoccupation with the author and text that characterizes the metafictional impulse in many postmodern narratives. These postmodern slave narratives move beyond the theoretical assertion that the historical representation of the past is "always already" subjective and therefore inaccessible to the human consciousness in any objective form. The fact that these writers claim narrative authority on the basis of their racial, cultural, ideological, and even experiential connection to their historical "subjects" flies in the face of postmodernist theoretical concepts that negate the autonomy of both author and text. From a "traditional" postmodernist perspective, the author can neither exist as a unified consciousness nor claim a stable racial or cultural identity. And yet, many writers of the postmodern slave narrative, drawing as they do from black nationalist and black feminist discourse, retain a fairly stable conception of cultural identity even across time. A coherent and substantive connection between the cultural experiences of the author and the historical subject remains central to a conception of narrative authority, and thus to retaining political agency.

Critics of postmodern thought ranging from black feminist writers like Collins to post-Marxist critics like Eagleton suggest that postmodernism, by destabilizing the individual subject and abstracting mechanisms of power, drains the capacity for effective political agency and mobilization. Many postmodern slave narratives circumvent this dilemma by using characters that reflect both the fragmented subjectivity of postmodernism and the political agency that black nationalists and black feminists view as an essential component of any discourse of resistance. In these narratives, slavery represents a historical moment when the African American self is both overdetermined and actively engaged in a project of liberation. The system of slavery interpellates the slave subject into a pervasive and inescapable process of subjugation. In these novels, as in the traditional slave narratives, the individual must confront the ways in which she has been enslaved by the real and identifiable social and political structure of American slavery. Although these texts establish slavery as an oppressive and hegemonic force, they also depict the slave's ability to liberate himself from this pervasive and oppressive ideological, political, and economic system. Within a cultural moment when traditional postmodernism proclaimed the fragmentation of the individual subject, the slave narrator/protagonist, both original and postmodern, stands as an example of individual agency and successful resistance. Far from a romanticized notion of individuality, postmodern slave narratives depict freedom as contested and wrought with conflict. Nevertheless, it is a freedom hard fought and won. As a narrative of resistance, most postmodern slave narratives refuse to posit the self as indeterminate in spite of the "overdetermination" of slavery.

If there is a historical continuity or political ideology implicit in these texts it is the narrative/ideology of resistance in the face of oppression. The postmodern slave narrative provides the contemporary reader with a model of individual and collective agency in the face of the interrelated forces of economic, political, racial, and cultural oppression. In this sense, contemporary writers retain the basic theme, structure, and function of the nineteenth century slave narrative. Just as the traditional slave narrative offered commentary on the cultural dilemmas of the nineteenth century, slave narratives of the late-twentieth-century turn to the past in an effort to re-form both the history and the historiography of the present. In spite of the fact that the postmodern slave narrative focuses on the historical institution of slavery, its re-formation of the past marks an interrogation of our postmodern condition. Contemporary African American writers suggest that our continuing conflicts with race, class, and gender has its roots in the Western ideology that created, developed, and perpetuated American slavery.

Although the novels I am calling postmodern slave narratives share a common sensibility toward the narrative act, they also tug at the nexus of discourses (postmodernism, black cultural nationalism, and black feminism) in unique ways and with varying results. It is as much my goal to emphasize the diversity of approaches and ideologies in these texts as it is to unite them. To this end, I have structured my chapters around concepts and formal strategies that, although all the texts share to some degree, some demonstrate more explicitly than others. In chapter 1, for example, I consider the manipulation of time in two contemporary slave narratives: Ishmael Reed's *Flight to Canada* and Octavia Butler's *Kindred*. Both Reed and Butler examine links between the nineteenth-century slave South and contemporary culture by blurring distinctions between the two time periods. Reed, through the frequent use of anachronistic references and cultural symbols, interrogates the relationship between slavery and contemporary commodity culture. Butler manipulates the convention of time travel by allowing her protagonist to move between two dimensions—1970s America and the antebellum South. To some extent, all postmodern slave narratives conflate past and present and, in the case of *The Gilda Stories* and *Stars in My Pocket like Grains of Sand,* they include the future in that conflation as well. Even Morrison's *Beloved,* which takes place primarily during the years just after slavery ended, develops a concept of rememory that asserts the physical presence of the past in the present.

Similarly, in chapter 2 I examine Morrison's *Beloved* through her use and critique of the gothic impulse. Morrison manipulates the symbolic dimensions of the gothic and places them in opposition to the historical detachment of traditional narrative history. In addition, Morrison's construction of Beloved as a character allows her to reinvent the conventions of the gothic novel by overtly politicizing this previously stylized and politically detached genre. A similar argument could be made for Jewelle Gomez's approach to the vampire tale or Octavia Butler's use of time travel in *Kindred.* However, Morrison's text explicitly shifts the foundations of the gothic novel by redefining the parameters of how we define what is "gothic" in the text.

As I suggested earlier, Charles Johnson's two novels, *Middle Passage* and *Oxherding Tale,* stake out an almost oppositional stance toward other postmodern slave narratives. Even as he reinvents the slave narrative form by infusing it with metafictional and allegorical dimensions, Johnson calls into question the very attempts of other postmodern slave narratives to claim narrative authority over the past. By rejecting stable definitions of racial identity but embracing an almost transcendental view of the power of fiction, Johnson's work stands in opposition to traditional history, black nationalism, postmodernism, and, perhaps most significantly, other postmodern slave narratives. Johnson's work sets the texts by Reed, Butler, and Morrison in bold relief and problematizes the figure of the slave narrator—a figure revered by these other authors. His novels suggest an alternative conception of black identity by drawing parallels between the intertextual dimensions of slave narratives and the process of transcultur-ation that occurred as a result of the Atlantic slave trade. In spite of his close adherence to the slave narrative form, Johnson rejects realism as much as other postmodern slave narratives by emphasizing the textuality of narrative history and of black identity itself.

Chapter 4 focuses on the treatment of slavery in Samuel R. Delany's science fiction novel *Stars in My Pocket like Grains of Sand* and Jewelle Gomez's *The Gilda Stories*. Rather than interrogating the past's relation-ship to the present, Delany and Gomez use the generic conventions of sci-ence fiction and the vampire tale, respectively, in order to extend their examinations of slavery into the future. Both Gomez and Delany explore post-slavery subjectivity within the conventions of their respective genres and, as a result, defamiliarize the postmodern slave narrative. In the process, both Delany and Gomez examine the ways the postmodern black subject must construct a community and a sense of identity in a world complicated by fragmentation, advanced technologies, and increasingly incoherent and multiple social systems.

Ultimately, what unites all of these texts and their writers is their rig-orous examination of what it means to construct a liberating conception of black identity in narrative form. That they turn to the history of slavery to do this reinforces the belief that, in order to create a liberating present, one must first liberate the constraints of the past. The strategies by which these writers go about this process may change but the goal and, unfortu-nately, the need remains the same.

The Conflation of Time in Ishmael Reed's *Flight to Canada* and Octavia Butler's *Kindred*

P ERHAPS the postmodern slave narrative's most fundamental re-
formation of the historiography of slavery occurs in its representation of time. In order to emphasize the links between past and present, contemporary African American writers create narratives that undermine conventions of linearity and distinctions between past and present.
In aesthetic terms, the expansiveness of speculative fiction and its rejection
of verisimilitude allow these writers to fashion a circular, or fluid, conception of time in their texts. By creating characters who occupy a world that
is both historical and contemporary, or that inexplicably travel through
time and space, writers of postmodern slave narratives challenge our
impulse to bury the past with willful ignorance or abstraction. In expanding the slave narrative's critique of slavery to include a critique of its legacy in contemporary America, African American writers emphasize the historical foundations of our current cultural condition. In this chapter I
focus on two contemporary slave narratives that most clearly manipulate
the elements of the fantastic in order to establish the connection between
past and present: Ishmael Reed's *Flight to Canada* and Octavia Butler's
Kindred. Though all of the narratives I examine in this book conflate time
in various ways, these two texts ground themselves firmly and explicitly in
both the antebellum South and late-twentieth-century America. These
texts continuously shift their treatment of the past and present, at
moments blurring the distinctions between time periods and, at others,
treating the history of slavery in its own context.

Although Butler and Reed both engage in a non-mimetic and nonlinear depiction of time and history, each conflates time through different thematic and formal means. In *Flight to Canada,* Ishmael Reed proliferates anachronisms in order to blur the distinctions between American slavery and late-twentieth-century commodity culture. The nineteenth-century characters in Reed's novel casually watch Lincoln's assassination on television, escape slavery by aircraft, and drive fancy automobiles. By incorporating these temporal incongruities into his text, Reed links the impulses behind the American slave system with the ways contemporary mainstream culture appropriates, commodifies, and consumes black identity and African American aesthetic production. The conflation of time also allows Reed to draw an explicit connection between the original slave narrators and contemporary black writers. Octavia Butler, in *Kindred,* conflates time in a far more physical and direct way; Dana Franklin, the novel's protagonist, acts as the anachronism that links the antebellum South with present-day America. Dana's experience of the past is *physical* as she inexplicably travels back and forth between her present-day life in post–civil rights Los Angeles and the rural Maryland landscape of the mid-nineteenth century, a culture in the throes of the American slave system. In order to ensure her own future existence, Dana must play an active role in the rape and impregnation of her great-grandmother at the hands of a white slave owner. Her confrontation with the past goes well beyond an intellectual or even emotional contemplation of her ancestral roots and ultimately plays itself out on the site of her body. As a result, Butler's novel emphasizes the physical and psychological links between slavery and contemporary American life. Dana's body and her ancestral ties act as physical sites of the past that she must confront in order to free herself from slavery and its legacy. Reed's novel, in its parodic manipulation of time and narrative convention, takes on a sardonic and satirical perspective on slavery and its legacy. As such, of the texts I examine in this study, it is the one most critics associate with other postmodernist fiction. By contrast, Butler's text de-emphasizes its fantastic dimensions in order to analyze the impact of slavery on the sexual politics of interracial relationships in the present. Rather than drawing attention to the ways Dana's time travel undermines the credibility of her slave experience, this element of the fantastic establishes her protagonist's truer, more complete understanding of slavery.

In spite of the differences both in tone and in the manipulation of fantastic elements, both Butler and Reed explicitly erase the boundaries between the past and the present, compelling readers to confront slavery, not as a distant and containable moment, but as a precursor to the present. Like Dana Franklin, readers of both texts are thrust from their contemporary perspectives into a crucial event in America's past. Neither Butler nor Reed, however, offers any rational explanation for the fissure of the natural boundaries of time and space in their novels. The unruly, even unpredictable, aspects of the past compel us to contemplate, however uncomfortably, the extent to which contemporary American culture remains rooted in American slavery. Whether we examine this past in terms of its commodification of black identity and black culture or in terms of its impact on interracial relationships, we must acknowledge it as an active, still evolving element of contemporary culture.

In essence, the postmodern slave narrative's orientation toward time grounds itself in the synchronic moment of slavery while simultaneously positing a diachronic view of time that acknowledges the past's continued resonance in the present. In synchronic terms, the postmodern slave narrative engages American slavery as a specific moment in the nation's history, one that reveals much about the values and morals of eighteenth- and nineteenth-century America. In diachronic terms, these texts emphasize the ideological foundations of American slavery that persist through time and cannot be isolated in one historical moment. This complex orientation toward time distinguishes postmodern slave narratives from traditional historical fiction. Historical novels such as *Gone with the Wind* or even Margaret Walker's *Jubilee* approach the historical past synchronically and remain firmly grounded in the specific historical periods the fictional narratives attempt to evoke. The postmodern slave narrative's primary goal, however, is to thematize its simultaneous occupation of two distinct time periods. Each time period informs the other in a mutual interchange, a mutual commentary.

The postmodern slave narrative's particular rejection of linear and mimetic representation also distinguishes it from similar excursions in white postmodern novels. By emphasizing the political and *material* links between slavery and contemporary culture, African American writers avoid abstract and indeterminate connections between past and present. As Brian McHale points out in *Postmodernist Fiction,* postmodern novels by white writers such as John Fowles's *The French Lieutenant's Woman* or Stanley Elkin's *George Mills* occupy multiple time periods through the use of "*creative* anachronism." McHale defines "creative anachronism" as a technique in which the contemporary sensibilities or worldview of the author or narrator offer commentary on the historical events of the text. In most cases, McHale argues, this manipulation of time "does not penetrate the fictional world but remains at the level of discourse, and the narrator, being our contemporary, is perfectly justified in making such allusions" (93). As it manifests itself in white postmodern novels, creative anachronism produces a disjuncture between the historical elements of the narrative by filtering them through the contemporary perspective of the author or narrator. As a result, only the abstract presence of an authorial figure provides commentary on the connections between the past and the present.[1] As a result, these novels investigate the past primarily as a discursive abstraction, raising questions about both the nature of historical reality itself and our ability to access that reality without the presence of narrative discourse.

In contrast to this abstract form of anachronism, McHale points out that one of the few examples of *material* anachronism occurs in Ishmael Reed's fiction, particularly in *Flight to Canada,* "where twentieth-century technology . . . is superimposed on nineteenth-century history" (93). Reed's use of material anachronism explicitly merges the past and the present periods beyond the level of discourse; physical objects mark contemporary culture and its relationship to the slave South. For Reed, anachronism extends well beyond its use as a literary device. The conflation of time in his work revolves around a particularly African conception of the past and its relation to the present; Reed asserts that "anachronism" is merely a literary term that fails to represent the cultural and spiritual relationship to time that lies behind his use of it. In an interview in 1977, Reed states:

> [A]ccording to *vodoun,* the past is contemporary. This is an element that many different African religions had in common. It was one of the guiding principles, in fact: the past *is* contemporary. In *Flight to Canada* I tried to make novelistic use of the concept, though everybody called it *anachronism,* after digging back into their literary glossaries. I was trying to work with the old *vodoun* theory of time. (Domini: 139)

Reed's invocation of the term "vodoun" reveals the influence of traditional African culture and spirituality. It expands on the black nationalist emphasis on the Afrocentric origins of black art. Reed's belief in a voodoo aesthetic that guides his own creativity foregrounds the multicultural and folkloric elements in his work which have their roots in both African and Native American culture.[2] Rather than a simple literary device, anachronism takes on ideological dimensions rooted in black nationalism, multiculturalism, and a postmodern critique of Eurocentrism. As such, the infusion of material anachronism in Reed's postmodern slave narrative represents more than a postmodern parody of the historiographical process; it is a fusion of ideological and cultural sensibilities that forms the basis of an African-influenced version of postmodernism.

Octavia Butler's *Kindred* distinguishes itself even further from the creative anachronisms of white postmodern fiction by constructing Dana, herself, as the anachronism of her text. Her material body is no longer limited to linear temporality. Both literally and symbolically, Dana's movement in time illustrates the fact that the past asserts itself in the present in a material and a physical way. When Dana returns to the present at the end of the novel, she loses her arm in the process. Far from an abstraction, Butler's text implies that the past permanently and inescapably scars us. Thus, the conflation of time in the postmodern slave narrative, as distinct from a purely creative form of anachronism, forces us to interrogate not only the discursive legacies of slavery in our contemporary moment but also the concrete and material connections between American slavery and late-twentieth-century culture. For both Reed and Butler, as well as for the characters they create within their texts, sharp distinctions between past and present are not only arbitrary, they negate the real value of returning to history in the first place. A conception of time that isolates the past from the present and vice versa undermines the political project of liberation. Only a narrative form that crosses those boundaries can resuscitate historical representations of slavery.

Commodity Culture and the Conflation of Time:
Ishmael Reed's *Flight to Canada*

From the opening pages of *Flight to Canada,* Ishmael Reed rejects the mimetic conventions of traditional historical representations of slavery and thrusts the reader into unfamiliar and disconcerting territory. The novel begins with a poem entitled "Flight to Canada," in which Raven Quickskill, the poem's author and the novel's protagonist, recounts his escape from slavery in bold and ironic strokes, making anachronistic references to "jumbo jets" and his ability to move freely between the North and the South. The poem marks Reed's initial use of material anachronism in conjunction with the infusion of a present-day worldview exemplified by Raven's assertive and signifying language:

I flew in non-stop
Jumbo jet this A.M. Had
Champagne Complements of the Cap'n
Who announced that a Runaway Negro was on the
Plane . . . Last visit I slept in
Your bed and sampled your Cellar. Had your prime
Quadroon give me She-bear. Yes, yes. (3–4)

Raven's poem is emblematic of Reed's own revision of the slave narrative. Both the novel and the poem re-form the slave narrative through a manipulation of time and a subversion of realism that opens up an alternative narrative space in which to represent the history of slavery. By conflating the antebellum South with post–civil rights America, Reed casts Raven's story as a version of his own. He forces readers to confront the relationship between the subjugation of African Americans under the system of slavery and the appropriation, commodification, and exploitation of black culture in contemporary America. The proliferation of anachronism allows Reed to equate his own situation as a black writer with Raven's as a slave narrator; their stories entwine in their mutual quest to achieve a liberating identity in the face of an oppressive economic and cultural system that seeks to contain, define, and exploit them. Reed's text moves beyond a mimetic and linear representation of the individual slave's quest for freedom and toward a re-formative and temporally fluid representation of the American slave system and its legacy in late-twentieth-century culture. Reed's text operates as a narrative act of liberation for both the escaped slave of the nineteenth century and the twentieth-century black artist.

The juxtaposition of the slave South and the postmodern condition in *Flight to Canada* functions ultimately as a critique both of the dominant culture's commodification of the slave narrative as a popularized depiction of the quest for freedom and its ensuing result: the commodification of the escaped slaves who constructed them. In re-forming the slave narrative through the conflation of time, Reed raises serious questions about the viability of any quest for a liberating identity. How can the slave narrator/black writer create the self through a medium marketed and controlled by the dominant and oppressive culture? How can the slave narrator/black writer hope to exploit a system designed to exploit those within it? Yet, rather than sacrificing the quest for a liberating, black identity in the face of these obstacles, Reed shifts the battlefield, transforming the slave narrative from a tale of liberation to a satirical critique of American commodity culture, past and present. Reed de-romanticizes conventional readings of the slave narrative as the individual slave's act of writing his or her self into being through the process of self-education and literacy. This ongoing narrative process re-forms the historical and cultural context of slavery.[3] This shift in focus from writing as a romantic act of defining one's humanity to writing as a form of cultural critique allows Reed not only to deconstruct the slave's quest for selfhood but also to indict the culture that would continuously and insidiously attempt to strip both the slave and the contemporary black artist of his identity.

Raven's assertion in the narrative section that opens the novel, "Little did I know when I wrote the poem 'Flight to Canada' that there were so many secrets locked inside its world. It was a reading more than a writing" (5), suggests that the act of writing may embody something much more than the romantic creation of the self. Raven's use of the word "reading" suggests that, first and foremost, the act of writing produces a reading of the world. While this is perhaps true of any artistic text, it is all the more true for the slave narrative, in both its original form and its postmodern revision. The slave narrative serves not only as an account of a slave's quest for freedom but also as an account of the slave system itself. Rather than a personal exploration of subjectivity, Raven's (and Reed's) emphasis on writing as an act of reading American culture produces a metafictional dimension in the text. In place of an easily digestible representation of the slave's flight from slavery to freedom, Reed creates a text that forces readers to interpret the temporal incongruities in the novel and to make connections between slavery and its persistent legacy in American culture.

Reed's emphasis on reading as a crucial component of the slave narrative, while a revision of the traditional form, still maintains a link to the original slave narratives. Houston Baker's reading of Frederick Douglass's 1845 *Narrative* foregrounds Douglass's skill as a reader and interpreter of texts when he writes:

> He [Douglass] refuses the role of hapless victim of texts (the slave master's false moral rhetoric) and becomes, instead, an astute interpreter and creator of texts of his own. . . . Douglass' acquired skills as reader enable him to provide his own interpretations of received texts. (43)

Douglass first must acquire and present a critical reading of slave culture before he can set about the task of narrating his own story. This process of developing his own critique of slavery, in turn, constitutes a fundamental dimension of his slave narrative—one that works in tandem with his romanticized creation of self through the written act. Rather than a complete reversal of the traditional slave narrative, Reed's narrative re-formation assumes the slave's humanity and focuses its attention on the constraints American commodity culture imposes upon that humanity.

Reed's rejection of a realistic and linear representation of the past also produces a critique of the original slave narrative as an aesthetic form and a commodifiable object. His revision is both parodic and pragmatic. It is infused with a late-twentieth-century sensibility informed by a postmodern critique of capitalism and a black nationalist critique of white mainstream culture's stultifying effect on black identity. From this African American postmodern perspective, Reed transforms the action of the slave narrative from the quest to achieve a previously unrealized humanity through literacy and perseverance to a quest for the almost impossible means of achieving freedom in a commodity culture by obtaining capital. The quest for freedom for the escaped slaves in *Flight to Canada* has less to do with reaching the North and more to do with successfully negotiating the market forces of capitalism without losing one's cultural identity. Reed deploys capitalism as both the means to obtain freedom and as the primary obstacle to that freedom

As the primary artist and narrator of the novel, Raven Quickskill illustrates the dangers commodity culture poses to the slave narrator to achieve freedom. More specifically, Raven's poem "Flight to Canada" represents the potential to exploit and the dangers of becoming exploited by a culture that views the slave narrative as not only a protest against slavery but also as a creative text for popular consumption. Though written before he fully attains his freedom, Raven's poem anticipates the rise of his celebrity status. In it he satirizes the ironic aspects of self-promotion that his participation in the abolitionist lecture circuit implies. He writes of people's reaction to his presence on the plane:

> Passengers came up
> And shook my hand
> & Within 10 min. I had
> Signed up for 3 anti-slavery
> Lectures. Remind me to get an
> Agent. (3)

Raven immediately exploits this process of commodification in order to escape slavery. Raven realizes that the literary representation of his escape will achieve instant commodity status, resulting less in the creation of a new identity as a free black man than in the creation of a product for consumption. The poem provides him with instant support from the anti-slavery movement and the economic means to obtain and maintain his freedom. Raven's glib references to getting an agent and signing up for anti-slavery lectures highlights the slave narrative's status as a cultural object that contains not only formal and aesthetic conventions but also maps a conventionalized relationship to its external means of production and consumption. Raven's text, just as Reed's, simultaneously manipulates this relationship and moves beyond the dominant culture's view of the slave narrative as an entertaining illustration and expression of his humanity. Through his satirical and mocking tone, Raven transforms the slave narrative and exploits its (and his) popular status for his own ends. Reed transforms Raven, as slave narrator, from the slave who achieves freedom through struggle and self-definition to the shrewd cultural player who manipulates market forces for social and financial gain.

As a player, Raven manipulates the stylistic conventions of the slave narrative and the economic and political forces that produce and define the text and its author. Initially, Raven exploits his newfound fame in the North as a result of the success and popularity of his poem. After escaping from slave owner Arthur Swille's plantation, Raven becomes a celebrity, speaking at anti-slavery lectures and even visiting the White House as a personal guest of Abe Lincoln. Upon his arrival in the North, Raven achieves star status equal to Walt Whitman, with whom he interacts during the formal reception at the White House. Clearly moving well beyond using the poem to establish his humanity, Raven uses the poem to defy the Fugitive Slave Law and to enter a society guided by its obsessive consumption of artistic texts and popular personalities. Raven plays the game of cultural commodities. He achieves the celebrity status that his own poem anticipated.

Reed elaborates on this simultaneously satirical and pragmatic view of the slave narrator by introducing William Wells Brown into the novel. Rather than the conventional and romantic image of the former slave, Brown in the novel represents the black writer who exploits capitalism from within the system. Reed replaces the image of the escaped slave who struggles to survive an equally hostile North with the image of the culturally savvy former slave who manipulates the complex cultural dynamics that converts his escape from slavery into a form of consumable entertainment. That Reed incorporates Brown into his novel, as opposed to other famous slave narrators such as Frederick Douglass or Henry Bibb, is significant in that Brown achieved widespread success both as a slave narrator and as an author of fiction.[4] Rather than succumbing to the pitfalls of consumer capitalism, William Wells Brown offers Raven a model of existence that turns the commodity culture back onto itself in order to achieve freedom, prosperity, and artistic success. Brown has achieved a status and freedom that other escaped slaves in the novel, including Raven, have yet to achieve, based primarily on his ability to tell his own story and manipulate the market that consumes it.

Upon their chance meeting in the novel, Raven names Brown, who appears confident and dashing in a "tall silk hat" and "black kid gloves," flashing business cards which describe him as an "Anti-Slavery Lecturer and Writer," as his main inspiration for the poem:

> I read your novel *Clotel* and . . . I just want to say Mr. Brown, that you're the greatest satirist of these times. . . . my poem "Flight to Canada" is going to be published in *Beulahland Review*. It kind of imitates your style, though I'm sure the critics are going to give me some kind of white master. A white man. They'll say he gave me the inspiration and that I modeled it after him. But I had you in mind. (121)

That Raven views *Clotel,* a novel generally regarded as one of the first fictional narratives by an African American to portray the tragedies and horrors of slavery, as a satire of the times and as a model for his own work establishes Reed's view of nineteenth-century textual production by black writers as a means to reflect and critique the culture of slavery through irony. While the white public for which the escaped slaves or free blacks write consumes these texts merely as melodramas or exposés on the tragic lives of enslaved African Americans, Raven (and ultimately Reed, himself) implies that these black writers also achieve a critical and aesthetic distance from their narratives. From this vantage point, black writers use irony and satire to interrogate the dominant culture that commodifies the black body and the black text. If we are to follow Raven's view of *Clotel,* and perhaps the work of other escaped slaves, these narratives critique the very discourse they reproduce. *Clotel,* with its melodramatic portrayal of tragic mulattos and the domestic upheavals caused by slavery, also stands as a critique of a culture that can only consume the horrors of slavery as melodrama. Brown's work serves as a precursor not only to Raven's poem but also to Reed's *Flight to Canada,* which frames it.

While Brown represents the successful manipulation of market forces, Reed also addresses the problems that could prevent the black writer (past and present) from achieving a liberating identity, even through this active form of resistance. One such problem is that the slave ultimately becomes a consumable object of pleasure for those who would enslave him. Simply put, as the dominant culture consumes his or her artistic text, the fugitive slave faces the prospect of "selling out." This is particularly true of the nineteenth-century slave narrator who must tell her story to a predominantly white consumer market. In order to appeal to that readership, the black writer, in an effort to increase consumption, must produce a representation of slavery that is accessible, and even desirable, to that audience. Reed suggests that, as representations of the slave experience become commodities consumed by members of the dominant culture, the black text replaces the black body as the commodified object of slavery. The process of commodification constitutes a re-enslavement of the black artist.

Raven realizes that by representing the black slave experience in his poem he enters a complex battlefield of economics, politics, and aesthetics, each entwined with the other. On one hand, Raven's poem allows him to assume an empowered position in spite of his status as a fugitive slave when he is thrust into the cultural limelight for his literary success. And yet, in his own pursuit of freedom in the novel and in his aesthetic representation of it, the poem also allows the dominant culture to contain and commodify his identity as an escaped slave. In essence, Raven's literary representation creates a paper trail by which his former master, Arthur Swille, and the forces of the slavocracy can not only capture him but can also constrain and define him.[5] Even after the Civil War has ended, Raven realizes that Swille will continue to pursue him. Although the physical shackles of slavery have been broken, the hegemony of cultural slavery still threatens to enslave him. It is this realization that leads to Raven's continued quest for his cultural and aesthetic freedom even after he achieves physical freedom when he reaches Canada.

In essence, Raven's flight to Canada represents a quest for liberation that goes beyond the physical and encompasses the cultural, economic, and aesthetic dimensions of slavery as an institution. In his quest, Raven encounters two characters who also attempt to subvert the multiple dimensions of slavery: Stray Leechfield, a friend of Raven Quickskill and formerly a fellow slave on Swille's plantation, and Quaw Quaw Tralaralara, a Native American woman and Raven's lover. Through his relationships with these characters, Raven begins to interrogate his own position as a commodity in a commodity culture. Leechfield and Quaw Quaw provide Raven with contrasting strategies of subverting cultural slavery and ultimately represent unsuccessful models in this quest. Raven, in response to these two approaches, constructs an alternative and oppositional aesthetic that critiques rather than conforms to the hegemony of American commodity culture. By conflating time through a proliferation of anachronisms, Reed establishes Leechfield and Quaw Quaw's preoccupation with cultural commodities and market forces as contemporary responses to slavery. On one hand, Stray Leechfield attempts to achieve freedom by manipulating the game of cultural commodities on purely economic terms. In the process, Leechfield ignores the implications and potentially degrading effects his representation will have on his narrative authority and political agency. On the other hand, Quaw Quaw Tralaralara attempts to transcend cultural slavery on purely aesthetic terms by creating a marketable and universal form of expression. Ultimately, her playful and abstract representations fail to achieve any political efficacy.

For Stray Leechfield, the foundation of American slavery has the same roots as the American Dream: economic prosperity. It is this belief that drives him to seek freedom through economic means; he works to buy his way from slavery.[6] In a conversation with Abe Lincoln, Arthur Swille describes with incredulity how Leechfield achieved prosperity even in slavery:

> He was stealing chickens—methodically. . . . He had taken so many over a period of time that he was over in the other county, big as you please, dressed up like a gentleman, smoking a seegar and driving a carriage which featured factory climate-control air conditioning, vinyl top, AM/FM stereo radio, full leather interior, power-lock doors, six-way power seat, power windows, white-wall wheels, door-edge guards, bumper impact strips, rear defroster and soft-ray glass. . . . He had set up his own poultry business, was underselling everybody in eggs, gizzards, gristles, livers—and had a reputation far and wide for his succulent drumsticks. He had a white slave fronting for him for ten percent. (36)

Leechfield's successful foray into the capitalist system allows him to leave, briefly, his position as a slave and enjoy the prosperity of entrepreneurialism. But Reed conflates Leechfield's economic resourcefulness as a slave with his flamboyant and materialistic display of twentieth-century consumerism. Leechfield's degeneration into consumer culture is embodied by the all-purpose status symbol: the luxury car. The intrusion of material anachronism in the text forces us to draw a connection between Leechfield's strategy for achieving freedom and contemporary consumerism. Through the accumulation of goods, Leechfield believes he can achieve freedom, prosperity, and class status. Leechfield ultimately succumbs to the excesses of commodity culture and fails to realize that, in spite of material prosperity, he remains a slave. When Swille's hired hand discovers that he has been stealing chickens and selling them, Leechfield must kill him and flee northward. Ultimately, Leechfield's manipulation of economics allows him only a limited sense of freedom; flight remains his only way out.

Once Leechfield establishes himself in the North, he must find another means of securing his freedom. When Raven escapes Swille's plantation and arrives in Emancipation City, he finds Leechfield in an office in an old warehouse marked "Leechfield & Leer." Upon entering the office, Raven describes, with horror and dismay, Leechfield's latest attempt to achieve prosperity in the face of cultural slavery:

> O my God! My God! My God! Leechfield was lying naked, his rust-colored body must have been greased, because it was glistening, and there was . . . there was—the naked New England girl was twisted about him, she had nothing on but those glasses and the flower hat. How did they manage? . . . The Immigrant [Leer] was underneath one of those Brady boxes—it was flashing. He . . . he was taking daguerreotypes, or "chemical pictures." (71)

Raven discovers that Leechfield has entered into the pornography business with Mel Leer, a Russian immigrant and former indentured servant. When he senses Raven's disapproval, Leechfield asserts, "Shit, everybody can't do anti-slavery lectures. I can't. I have to make it the best I can, man. I don't see no difference between what I'm doing and what you're doing" (72). In an effort to make enough money to buy himself from Swille, Leechfield commodifies his own body. On one level, this commodification can be seen as a direct manipulation of the dominant culture's preoccupation with the stereotypical and sexually degrading dimensions of slavery. However, on another level, Leechfield, in spite of the fact that he has escaped the physical bonds of slavery, still degrades and commodifies his body in the pornographic depiction of the slave experience. From Leechfield's perspective, fetishizing the slave experience in pornographic pictures is analogous to Raven's reconstruction of slavery in his poems and anti-slavery lectures: each commodifies slavery in an attempt to profit from its popular representation. To regard the act of recounting the horrors of slavery and the individual quest for freedom as a marketable resource opens the door for any version of the slave's self to be regarded as a fetishized commodity, whether it is the sexualized image of Leechfield's black body or Raven's textualized persona of the escaped slave. For Leechfield, the main purpose is to achieve the economic means to buy freedom; the particular form and content of his aesthetic representation remains a superfluous afterthought.

If Stray Leechfield represents a one-dimensional view of slavery on economic terms, Quaw Quaw Tralaralara, the popular and sensationalist Native American tightrope artist, represents the limitations of escaping cultural slavery on purely abstract and aesthetic terms. In a conversation with Raven, Quaw Quaw argues that "slavery is a state of mind, metaphysical" and that Raven's approach to his own art is too limited in conception. She states: "You're just not broad enough Quickskill. You're . . . you're too . . . too ethnic. You should be more universal. . . . Politics. Race. People write and paint about politics because they have nothing else to say" (95–96). It is from this vantage point that Quaw Quaw constructs her own performance art as a means to achieve popularity and cultural success. When Raven encounters her in Canada, he sees her performing her brand of universal aesthetics to much fanfare and excitement:

> She was in Indian clothes. . . . She was walking a tightrope across Niagara Falls. . . . Carrying the banner she did a somersault. The crowd gaped and murmured. She kept coming across the tightrope as the crowd on both sides grew hushed. It seemed that the Falls had hushed. . . . She reached the other side and the crowd went wild, joining hands and jumping about, whistling, stomping their feet. (156–57)

Quaw Quaw literally and figuratively walks a tightrope between a personalized expression of her identity and a sensationalist pastiche. The audience she reaches consumes her tightrope act as a flamboyant display in the tradition of sideshow and circus acts rather than as an expression of any cultural tradition. It is a universal aesthetic only insofar as it projects a quality of nothingness—an absence of substance that epitomizes sheer sensationalism. Raven ultimately criticizes Quaw Quaw for being an "ambitious mountain climber" and for selling short her own cultural heritage.

Just as Leechfield fails to realize the hegemonic power of cultural slavery by focusing on economics, Quaw Quaw, in her attempts at achieving a universalism through sensationalism, fails to interrogate the ways in which the dominant culture consumes and commodifies her art. And in the process of this commodification, the dominant culture restricts and obscures her cultural identity. In response to Quaw Quaw's suggestion that his art should be more universal and less political, Raven points out that slavery has its roots in the links between aesthetics and politics:

> What Camelot can't win on the battlefield it'll continue in poetry. . . . They're going to get your Indian and my Slave on microfilm and in sociology books; then they're going to put them in the spaceship and send them to the moon. And then they're going to put you on the nickel and put me on a stamp, and that'll be the end of it. They're as Feudalist and Arthurian as [Jefferson] Davis, but whereas he sees it as a political movement, they see it as a poetry movement. (96)

Quaw Quaw's attempts to create a liberating identity through her tight-rope act and pretensions toward universalism ultimately fail to free her from the hegemony of capitalism and the dominant culture. Both Leechfield and Quaw Quaw acknowledge only one dimension of their oppression and fail to engage slavery through the complex links between aesthetics, economics, and politics. More than just economic and physical enslavement, Reed's construction of Quaw Quaw and Leechfield suggests that, through a system of commodification, the mainstream American culture seeks to define and confine minority cultures as consumable objects.

The dilemma of the black artist and the seemingly insurmountable mountain of cultural slavery compel Raven to pursue a more liberating means by which he can tell his story in the face of a hegemonic commodity culture. Raven initially believes that the way he can achieve cultural freedom is through his own visionary aesthetic and creative power:

> While others had their tarot cards, their ouija boards, their I-Ching, their cowrie shells, he had his "writings." They were his bows and arrows. He was so much against slavery that he had begun to include prose and poetry in the same book, so that there would be no arbitrary boundaries between them. He preferred Canada to slavery, whether Canada was exile, death, art, liberation, or a woman. . . ."Flight to Canada" was responsible for getting him to Canada. And so for him, freedom was his writing. His writing was his HooDoo. Others had their way of HooDoo but his was his writing. It fascinated him, it possessed him; his typewriter was his drum he danced to. (88–89)

By blurring the boundaries between poetry and prose, between fiction and history, Raven attempts to create both a personalized expression of his experience and a satire of the times. "Flight to Canada" marks his attempt to create a text that reinscribes and reinvests the representation of slavery with a creative and critical power. Itself a mixture of prose and poetry, of the historical with the fictional, Ishmael Reed's *Flight to Canada* also marks a significant departure from the standard conventions of the slave narrative. According to Joe Weixlmann, Reed produces "an overt representation of freedom" by constructing the novel as "diversity-in-action" (65). In this sense, Reed, like Raven, explodes the slave narrative form and achieves a kind of "aesthetic Canada" through the liberation of artistic vision. Both the poem and the novel in "theme and form combine to produce empowered and empowering objects that deny both facile categorization and promote a genuine sense of literary and sociopolitical freedom" (67).

And yet, even Raven's attempts at liberation through his defamiliarizing and (re)visionary literary form could potentially succumb to the consumptive powers of commodity culture. In true postmodernist fashion, Reed turns to another historical literary figure to point out the dangers black writers face in having their stories appropriated by the white literary establishment. In the opening section of the novel (entitled "Naughty Harriet"), Reed indicts Harriet Beecher Stowe for her appropriation of Josiah Hensen's story for her famous novel *Uncle Tom's Cabin*:

> The story she "borrowed" from Josiah Hensen. Harriet only wanted enough money to buy a silk dress. The paper mills ground day and night. She'd read Josiah Hensen's book. That Harriet was alert. The Life of Josiah Hensen, Formerly a Slave. Seventy-seven pages long. It was short, but it was his. It was all he had. His story. A man's story is his gris-gris, you know. Taking his story is like taking his gris-gris. The thing that is himself. (8)

According to Richard Walsh, this act of plagiarism, which provides the fuel for the novel's interrogation of cultural slavery, "stands for the cultural appropriation by which minority cultures are suppressed and for the subsequent oppression of their people, the essence of Reed's metaphor of slavery" (66–67). I would argue that Reed's conflation of time elevates this from pure metaphor into a level of direct critique of a culture that continues to appropriate black subjectivity through its literary texts.

Reed further complicates the political, economic, and aesthetic nexus of cultural slavery through the character Yankee Jack, successful businessman and Quaw Quaw's husband. Known as the "Good Pirate," Yankee Jack builds Emancipation City, a refuge for escaped slaves, and fashions himself as a distributor of cultural objects and artifacts. But behind Yankee Jack's marriage to Quaw Quaw and his seemingly benevolent interest in the affairs of escaped slaves in Emancipation City lies his sinister role in the subjugation of oppressed peoples. In his poem "The Saga of Third World Belle," Raven exposes Yankee Jack's murder of Quaw Quaw's father and the pillaging of her culture:

> Your favorite pirate uses
> Your Dad's great chief's skull
> As an ashtray
> And sold your Mom's hand-knitted
> Robes to Buffalo Bill's Wild West Show.
>
> He buried your brother alive
> In a sealed-off section of the Metropolitan Museum. (123)

If Stowe stands as a symbol for cultural appropriation in the text as Richard Walsh suggests, Yankee Jack represents the *agent* of cultural commodification, exploitation, and appropriation, nullifying black identity by containing, marketing, and belittling it. For Reed, Yankee Jack embodies the oppressive vehicle of cultural commodification hidden beneath the surface benefits of exploiting this system. Beyond exploiting the economics of commodification, Yankee Jack exerts control over minority culture from a dominant position. Raven confronts Yankee Jack about his role in the cultural enslavement of minorities, stating:

> You call yourself a "distributor," attempting to make yourself respectable. You decide which books, films, even what kind of cheese, no less, will reach the market. At least we fuges know we're slaves, constantly hunted, but you enslave everybody. Making saps of them all. You, the man behind a distribution network, remaining invisible while your underlings become the fall guys. (146)

Reed's portrayal of Yankee Jack suggests that he is the symbol of capitalism itself, guided solely by the prospect of profit. But, ultimately, as Yankee Jack himself points out, he is just a middleman protecting the dictates of the dominant culture from a position of power. It is the position of dominance itself that allows him to commodify minority cultures and to determine which cultural expressions are civilized and which are savage.

With all the obstacles and potential pitfalls of cultural commodification, the process of creating a liberating black identity by writing the self into being or by exploiting the effects of commodification on purely economic or aesthetic terms becomes a seemingly impossible enterprise. Clearly the production of the slave narrative specifically and the black artistic text in general needs to involve more than a romanticized notion of identity, a false and oversimplified conception of universality, or a pre-occupation with the accumulation of wealth. Reed's subversive and fantastic re-formation of the slave narrative (as symbolized by Raven's own radical revision of the form) presents the reader with an alternative strategy for achieving a form of creative and artistic freedom. By defamiliarizing the history of slavery, deromanticizing the quest for freedom, and conflating past and present, Reed forces readers to reconceptualize the figure of the slave narrator and the cultural discourse that surrounds the slave narrative both original and postmodern.

At this point I must return to Reed's emphasis on active *reading* as a fundamental component of the slave narrative. This concept works on two levels. First, it highlights the fact that as the creator of the slave narrative, the author (Douglass, Reed, and even Raven as a fictional author) produces his own critical reading of the cultural context of slavery. Second, the written text as reading must, in turn, produce additional readings as it is consumed and interpreted as a cultural text. What Reed makes clear through his explicit inclusion of the consumptive act of reading and the productive act of interpretation into his novel is the fact that these functions operate under the same potentially oppressive system of capitalism as the act of writing. Just as Reed faces the dilemma of being exploited by commodity culture like Raven, his fictional counterpart, so too does the reader face the prospect of complicity in that exploitation. Like the symbol of appropriation, Harriet Beecher Stowe, and the agent of capitalism, Yankee Jack, the reader's consumption of the text creates the possibility of tracking down the black artist by commodifying blackness and, therefore, undermining the potentially liberating function of the text.

As Robert Elliot Fox points out, the poem "Flight to Canada" "symbolizes, for Reed, the way misinformed criticism 'catches' or categorizes black artists" (71). By shifting the focus from a romanticized creation of the self as the primary liberating function of the slave narrative to a politicized critique of commodity culture, Reed presents the reader with a text that defies conventional consumption and interpretation. By forcing readers to resolve the continuous temporal incongruities in the text, Reed shifts the object of consumption and critique away from black identity and toward the culture (past and present) that commodifies both the black text and the black body. It is only by rejecting the conventions of realism and the linearity of traditional history that Reed can achieve liberation through the slave narrative form. The conflation of time in the novel ultimately functions as a narrative conceit and as an assertion of Reed's authority to equate the dilemmas of the contemporary black writer with his literary precursor: the slave narrator. As we will see in *Kindred,* Octavia Butler extends this conceit even further by drawing on the convention of fantastic or speculative fiction. In her text, even more than in Reed's, the boundaries of time and space lose their integrity, thus opening the door for a radical re-formation of the discourse on slavery. Such a gesture allows Butler to forge a link between the contemporary subject and the subject of history.

Time Travel and the Anachronistic Subject in Octavia Butler's *Kindred*

The most crucial difference between the ways Octavia Butler and Ishmael Reed conflate time in their texts is the effect this conflation has on both the characters they construct and the readers they engage. In *Flight to Canada,* Reed's narrative initially disorients the reader through a profusion of material and creative anachronisms. And yet, as the anachronisms proliferate, our ability to occupy the present and the past within the novel becomes seamless; we begin to see the relationship between the contemporary and the historical as fluid. This is due, in large part, to the fact that, even as certain elements of the text defy linear and temporal logic, Raven Quickskill and the other characters stand firmly grounded in the antebellum South. As they accept the reality of that past as bearing the mark of the present, we too, as readers, accept the relationship between American slavery and contemporary commodity culture. In contrast, Butler's erasure of the boundaries between time and space occur much more violently for both her protagonist and, in narrative terms, her readers. By displacing time across the physical and psychological planes of Dana's identity, Butler creates a narrative in which the conflation of time has damaging and lasting effects. As a result, the parodic and sometimes humorous effect we see in Reed's text disappears in favor of a disconcerting and often disturbing confrontation with temporal displacement and the history of slavery.[7]

By incorporating time travel, one of the common tropes of science fiction, Butler establishes the movement between past and present as the central event of her novel. Yet, unlike Reed, who examines the relationship between slavery and contemporary culture through the figurative and formal structures of his text, Butler examines this link in a literal fashion. Even as she gestures toward the "unreality" of time travel, Butler strives to maintain a realistic representation of nineteenth-century slavery. In this regard, *Kindred*, unique among Butler's other fiction, resembles traditional historical fiction more than science fiction. Much like the original slave narratives, Butler structures her novel as a first-person retrospective account of Dana's flight from enslavement to freedom. The juxtaposition of the fantastic with the "real" (in terms of narrative mimesis) has a disruptive effect in the novel. In essence, *Kindred* is a hybrid narrative that combines the realism of traditional historical fiction, the basic structure of the slave narrative, and the thematic elements of fantastic literature. By fusing these divergent forms in her novel, she transforms each of these genres and their conventions in a uniquely postmodern re-formation of the slave narrative.

Kindred centers on Dana's inexplicable and unpredictable movements through time from her present life in Los Angeles circa 1976 to the slave plantation where her great-grandmother Alice Greenwood and her white ancestor, Rufus Weylin, will begin her family line. The first time Dana travels into the past occurs when Rufus, as a child, almost drowns in a river. Dana finds herself transported from her living room and into the rural Maryland landscape. She instinctively responds to the young boy's screams for help, pulling him from the river and reviving him. When Rufus's father, Tom Weylin, threatens her life at gunpoint, Dana loses consciousness and returns to the present. In spite of her initial disbelief after her first experience of time travel, Dana soon intuits that she has been thrust into the past in order to insure that Rufus and Alice begin the family line by giving birth to her grandmother Hagar. Upon her second encounter with the past she makes this connection:

> I looked over at the boy who would be Hagar's father. There was nothing in him that reminded me of my relatives. Looking at him confused me. But he had to be the one. There had to be some kind of reason for the link he and I seemed to have.... What we had was something new, something that didn't even have a name. Some matching strangeness in us that may or may not have come from our being related. . . . Was that why I was here? Not only to insure the survival of one accident-prone young boy, but to insure my family's survival, my own birth. (28–29)

At various points throughout Rufus's life, Dana travels into the past and builds a complicated and tenuous relationship with her white ancestor. Besides enduring the perils of being a black woman in the slave South, Dana's ultimate dilemma is the role she must play in Rufus's rape of her great-grandmother. In this sense, Dana's investment in the past is deeply personal—she must come to terms with the sexual violence and oppression that mark her own existence.

In an interview with Randall Kenan, Butler suggests that the conflation of time in *Kindred* arose out of a desire both to confront the past and to respond to the present, stating:

> *Kindred* was a kind of reaction to some of the things going on in the sixties when people were feeling ashamed of, or more strongly, angry with their parents for not having improved things faster, and I wanted to take a person from today and send that person back to slavery. (496)

The fact that Butler dates the impetus of the novel in the sixties suggests that *Kindred* is a response to the Black Arts and Black Power movements which emphasized resistance to white domination and rejected integrationist attitudes toward white culture. At times this radical stance resulted in a rejection of black writers and cultural figures that displayed integrationist political or aesthetic stances. As a response to this radical dimension of black nationalism, Butler uses elements of the fantastic to force those who harshly criticize their parents (and perhaps their enslaved ancestors as well) into an active and visceral confrontation with the hardships of slavery and racial oppression in direct terms. The contemporary events of the text, however, actually take place several years later during the summer of 1976, which coincides with the American bicentennial. As such, the novel casts the bicentennial in an ironic light, emphasizing historical realities of slavery in the midst of the nation's celebration of two hundred years of independence. The conflation of time allows Butler to inform both mainstream America and advocates of black nationalism that the legacy of slavery still marks the nation's history and manifests itself in the physical and psychological wounds of the present. The juxtaposition of America's two-hundredth birthday and the racial struggle grounded in the civil rights and Black Power movements allows the novel to occupy multiple social and historical contexts, at once evoking a critique of the patriotism of mainstream America and the radicalism of black nationalism.

In the midst of these competing contemporary and historical contexts, Butler places Dana Franklin at the center of the novel's cultural and temporal maelstrom. In many ways, Dana represents a perfect link between the multiple time frames and the conflicting sociopolitical views of the Black Power movement and white mainstream America. In Dana Franklin, Butler constructs a character who has embedded herself in the racial politics of contemporary America and yet has maintained an ambiguous stance in relation to these politics. She is willing to acknowledge the pervasive racism that marks American culture even as she attempts to transcend that racism in her personal life. Dana's marriage to Kevin, a white man, and her relative silence about specific racial or political issues suggest that she places herself outside the political discourse of black nationalism and supports an integrationist view of American culture. Although Dana does not view her marriage as a political statement, she does acknowledge the complexities that surround interracial relationships in a culture struggling with racial tension and inequity. As such, Dana stands betwixt and between the radical politics of the Black Power movement, the integrationist stance suggested by her marriage to Kevin, and the racism that her status as a black woman and her marriage to Kevin inspires. The complexities of Dana's present life prevent us from interpreting her movement through time merely as the isolated experience of one individual or as simply an element of science fiction. Rather, Butler's treatment of time travel stands as a powerful exploration of racial politics in America, both past and present.

Octavia Butler's use of the fantastic as a vehicle for conflating the past and the present raises many questions as to the nature of the relationship between slavery and contemporary America. Why is it that the past intrudes so violently upon Dana's life in the present? What connections must Dana make between her contemporary life and the past experiences of her ancestors? What effect do Dana's experiences in the past have on her life in the present? The central challenge of the text lies in our answers to these crucial questions. As Dana struggles with the interconnections between her enslavement in the past and the volatility of her life in the present, we must come to terms with the echoes of slavery that persist in contemporary American culture. As such, our reading of *Kindred* hinges upon the ways we negotiate Butler's conflation of time and the ambiguities she generates through her narrative manipulation of one of the basic tropes of science fiction.

From the outset of the novel, Butler disrupts the reader's orientation toward time not only by transporting Dana into the past but also by leaving crucial aspects of her time travel unexplained. These ambiguities complicate the reader's interpretation of Dana's relationship to her own ancestral past. On the most basic level, Butler never explains how Dana passes back and forth between her present life in California and the Maryland plantation in the past. Butler herself argues that the ambiguity surrounding the means for Dana's time travel places *Kindred* outside the genre of science fiction.[8] Other than Dana's time travel, Butler maintains a realistic

representation of the past and avoids the metaphysical or technical preoccupations with time travel that are normally associated with traditional science fiction. By constructing this fantastic event in ambiguous and yet realistic terms, Butler challenges us to interpret its presence not as an aspect of
science fiction or through a suspension of disbelief but, rather, as a narrative conception of time that links Dana's present reality with the lives of her
ancestors. In the absence of a "scientific" explanation, Butler replaces the
question of *how* Dana travels through time with the more crucial question
of *why* such a physical intersection between past and present exists for her.

In addition to the ambiguity surrounding Dana's movement through
time, Butler also leaves the first moment of Dana's confrontation with the
past ambiguous. Dana states in the first chapter: "The trouble began long
before June 9, 1976, when I became aware of it, but June 9th is the day I
remember. It was my twenty-sixth birthday. It was also the day I first met
Rufus—the day he called me to him the first time" (3). Though her movement through time constitutes the most obvious disruption in her life, the
opening lines suggest the central crisis of her life lies outside her time travel. Neither Butler nor Dana elaborate on the implications of Dana's trouble
having begun long before her first movement through time. The fact that
Butler leaves the origins and causality of Dana's time travel ambiguous
opens the door to several possible interpretations as to the reasons why the
past invades her life in such a disruptive and dangerous manner. I would
argue that these ambiguities, these competing interpretations of when "the
trouble" begins for Dana, set the stage for the novel's treatment of time.
Much as the proliferation of anachronism in Reed's text compels readers to
re-examine the nature of time and history in narrative, the open-endedness
of Butler's novel forces us to assume an active role in examining the relationship between the past and the present in general, and the relationship
between nineteenth-century slavery and late-twentieth-century America.

If Dana's trouble begins long before her first *physical* confrontation with
the past, her limited knowledge of American slavery offers one possible
explanation for her time travel. Though Dana most certainly is aware of the
history of American slavery before she actually travels into the past, her
knowledge of that past is abstract and distant, obscured by the passage of
over one hundred years since the end of slavery. Dana's alienation from this
crucial component of her own history may function as some kind of contemporary crisis that triggers her physical encounter with slavery. Butler's
statement that her novel is a response to the critical attitudes some African
Americans had toward their parents suggests that the "trouble" may, in fact,
refer to the limited ways we conceptualize the history of slavery from a

late-twentieth-century or early-twentieth-first-century vantage point. Butler suggests that these criticisms stem from a lack of awareness of the difficulties African Americans had to endure through American history. From this standpoint, Dana's violent confrontation with the past and Butler's construction of it serve as a means to deepen her (and ultimately our) understanding of slavery and racial struggle beyond the abstract, distant, and seemingly objective knowledge disseminated by official history. The novel instructs us, in a more direct and visceral fashion, on the hardships that slaves had to endure in order to survive. Dana's life in the past enables her to identify with the specific circumstances of her ancestors and the violence of slavery beyond the limitations of traditional history. Dana's time travel allows her to develop a concrete connection to her personal and cultural history through direct interaction with her ancestors.

The fact that Dana identifies the trouble as beginning before her first encounter with Rufus suggests that the events that established her own ancestry—the specific events that she encounters in the past—cause the disruption in linear time. If the crisis of her ancestry causes Dana's physical confrontation with slavery, it would suggest that Rufus's rape of Alice is a defining moment for Dana, even in her contemporary life. On a psychological level, Dana's time travel comes out of her present need to confront the violence and oppression that informs her ancestry. But what are the implications of Butler's suggestion that the circumstances of Dana's ancestry function as the central crisis of her contemporary existence? If the trouble refers to Rufus's rape of Alice in the past, then the novel implies that Dana's own life, her relationship with Kevin, and her place in contemporary America are indelibly connected to this moment in her family's history. Rufus's violent and oppressive relationship with Dana's great-grandmother Alice, certainly one of the dominant models of sexual relationships between white men and black women during American slavery, plays a major role in the way we view the history of interracial relationships between blacks and whites in contemporary America. If the trouble begins with Rufus's rape of Dana's great-grandmother, Butler suggests that Dana must interrogate the current racial tensions that mark her relationship with Kevin through an intimate understanding of its roots in her own past.

Dana's interracial relationship with Kevin in the present also suggests that the specific events in her current life, as much as the events of her ancestral past, play a role in Dana's "trouble." At the time of the narrative, Dana has recently married and moved in with Kevin after a brief courtship. Both orphans and struggling writers, Kevin and Dana quickly develop a serious relationship based on their similar interests and their sense of isolation in the world. Their relationship, however, causes tension between Dana and her only living relatives: her aunt and uncle. In turn, Kevin's sister, his only living relative, refuses to acknowledge his relationship with Dana. Because of the persistent intolerance toward interracial relationships, both Dana and Kevin find themselves estranged and isolated from their families. If Dana identifies her alienation from her aunt and uncle as the source of her trouble, it implies that the main issue she must confront is the role the legacy of slavery has played in both her relationship with Kevin and the isolation she must endure because of her marriage to him. Dana's central dilemma, then, lies not only in ensuring her ancestral line in the past but also in coming to terms with the contemporary racial, social, and familial ramifications of her marriage to Kevin.

Over the course of the narrative, Dana's reaction to the past implies a hierarchy in terms of the way she, and perhaps we as readers, confronts the legacy of slavery. Dana responds to the connections between the past and the present on four different levels ranging from the ways the legacy of slavery has marked contemporary American culture to the ways in which it has inscribed itself on the internal dimensions of individual identity. By constructing these connections in this way, Butler suggests that slavery informs our contemporary moment in many ways, but perhaps most profoundly in its continuing impact on the self. On the first level, Dana's experience of the physical violence of slavery allows her to draw comparisons between slavery as an institution and other oppressive political systems in recent history. On the second level, Dana confronts the connection between her life as an impoverished, twentieth-century black woman and her life as a slave forced into labor for the profit of her enslavers. On a deeper level, Dana must acknowledge the connections between the patriarchal dimensions of her relationship with Kevin in the present and her complex interactions with Rufus and his father, Tom Weylin, in the past. Finally, Dana must also come to terms with the profound connections between herself and Alice Greenwood, her spiritual and biological ancestor. As the links between the two time periods begin to touch her on progressively deeper psychological levels, the parallels between Dana's life in the slave South and her life in present-day Los Angeles begin to intersect and become more difficult to resolve.

Initially, Dana's experiences in the past allow her to draw parallels between the institution of slavery and other twentieth-century examples of oppression and subjugation. Though these comparisons lie on a broad cultural level and have little to do with her own life in the present, Dana's first-hand experience of the physical atrocities of slavery allows her to understand the experiences of others who have endured similar atrocities. In her first two encounters with slavery, Dana tries to maintain a distance between her contemporary self and the events she experiences in the past.[9] It is a distance, however, that proves impossible to maintain. During her third confrontation with the past, Dana gains a concrete understanding of the violence used to subjugate her enslaved ancestors. When Tom Weylin catches her teaching two enslaved children how to read, he whips her. For the first time, Dana must physically endure the violence of slavery. Fearing that her life is in danger, Dana loses consciousness. With this experience of slavery imprinted on her mind and scarred on her body, Dana returns, albeit briefly, to the present, armed with a unique perspective on the past. In an effort to contextualize her experiences in the past, Dana turns to the historical texts she owns in the present. However, the texts she finds, particularly those on slavery, are woefully inadequate:

> I read books about slavery, fiction and nonfiction. I read everything I had in the house that was even distantly related to the subject—even *Gone with the Wind,* or part of it. But its version of happy darkies in tender loving bondage was more than I could stand. Then, somehow I got caught up in one of Kevin's World War II books—a book of excerpts from the recollections of concentration camp survivors. Stories of beatings, starvation, filth, disease, torture, every possible degradation. As though the Germans had been trying to do in only a few years what the Americans had worked at for nearly two hundred. The books depressed me, scared me, made me stuff Kevin's sleeping pills in my bag. Like the Nazis, ante bellum whites had known quite a bit about torture—quite a bit more than I ever wanted to learn. (116–17)

Weylin's brutality gives Dana knowledge of slavery and oppression that traditional narratives cannot replicate. The only texts on slavery to which Dana has immediate access not only limit her understanding of her own experience but misrepresent the historical realities of slavery. As a result, Dana must turn to a more recent corollary to illuminate her own past: the torture of Jews in Nazi Germany. Her direct confrontation with the violence of slavery allows her to understand this connection across racial, political, and cultural lines. And this connection comes largely as a result of her need to contextualize the violence that has marked her body.

Another example of the connections Dana makes between the past and twentieth-century life occurs after she returns from her fourth experience in the antebellum South. Dana slowly loses herself in the events of the past and begins to find it increasingly difficult to acclimate herself to life in 1976. In an effort to connect herself to current events in her own time, Dana turns on a radio news program. After a report on America's military conflict in Lebanon, the news story switches to the continuing racial conflict in apartheid South Africa. The description of these events disturbs Dana and forces her to make a connection between racial oppression in the twentieth century with the white culture that exploits and enslaves her ancestors in the nineteenth century:

> I turned off the radio and tried to cook the meal in peace. South African whites had always struck me as people who would have been happier living in the nineteenth century, or the eighteenth. In fact, they were living in the past as far as race relations went. They lived in ease and comfort supported by huge numbers of blacks whom they kept in poverty and held in contempt. (196)

However contemporary Americans might seek to relegate the atrocities of human subjugation to a past that has ended, it is clear from the conflict in South Africa that the basic ideology of racial oppression endures in many forms. Dana can identify with its persistence in current political situations as a result of her direct experience with the past.

Dana also makes connections between her life as a late-twentieth-century black woman and the lives of her ancestors living in the slave South. These parallels relate more closely to Dana's own life in the present and move beyond a reflection of the broader political manifestations of the Western impulse to oppress and subjugate groups of people it classifies as "other." On this more personal level, Dana draws distinct parallels between the ways she has experienced racism and racial oppression in her present life and the way she has experienced them in the past. One example of this comparison occurs when she describes her experiences working for a labor agency, which she refers to as a "slave market." Dana draws on her experience in the past and the present to point out how the legacy of slavery informs class issues and employment practices in contemporary America. In this instance, Dana notes that poverty and class exploitation are modern corollaries to slavery:

> I was working out of a casual labor agency—we regulars called it a slave market. Actually, it was the opposite of slavery. The people who ran it couldn't have cared less whether or not you showed up to do the work they offered. They had more job hunters than jobs anyway. . . . Getting sent out

meant the minimum wage—minus Uncle Sam's share—for as many hours as you were needed. You swept floors, stuffed envelopes, took inventory, washed dishes, sorted potato chips (really!), cleaned toilets, marked prices on merchandise . . . you did whatever you were sent out to do. It was nearly always mindless work, and as far as employers were concerned, it was done by mindless people. Nonpeople rented for a few hours, a few days, a few weeks. It didn't matter. (52–53)

Dana's contemporary experience of poverty and low-wage employment serves as a precursor to her experiences working in the fields of the Weylin plantation as a slave in the past. The dehumanizing aspect of working as cheap labor, of using her body as a commodity for those who care little for her individual identity, allows Dana to draw an explicit connection between the commodification of Africans as slaves and the exploitation of the underclass in contemporary America.

The connections between her interactions with white males in the past and her relationship with Kevin, however, provide Dana and the readers with a more personally profound corollary between her experiences in the past and her contemporary life. Dana's encounters with Tom and Rufus Weylin, in particular, force her to confront the complexities of interracial relationships in the wake of slavery and racial oppression. As Lucie Armit argues, because Rufus controls Dana's time travel, calling her to the past whenever his life is in danger, "it is the patriarchal pull of the linear that remains the dominant structural force in the novel" (54). In this sense, Rufus stands as the dominant patriarchal figure of Dana's past life. One of Dana's main dilemmas in the nineteenth century, then, is to come to terms with her ambivalence toward Rufus as she repeatedly saves his life in order to ensure her own existence. In the present, Kevin stands as the dominant patriarchal figure in Dana's life. Though Kevin plays (in large part) a positive and supportive role in Dana's life, he also generates a degree of ambivalence in Dana. Not only does her marriage to him cause a rift in her relationship with her only living relatives, but Kevin also demonstrates some tendencies toward her that reflect his patriarchal desire to control her in their marriage. As Dana's encounters with the past progress, the conflicts that arise out of her connection with Rufus begin to reflect the tensions in her marriage to Kevin. The conflation of past and present forces Dana to confront her ambivalence toward Rufus as her ancestor in order to come to terms with the complexities of her interracial relationship with Kevin.

Most of the comparisons Dana draws between Kevin and the white slave owners of the nineteenth century are superficial, yet disturbing. On a purely physical level, Dana notices a resemblance between Tom Weylin and her husband. During her second encounter with the past, Dana feels uncomfortable when Weylin stares at her, sizing her up. She states: "His eyes, I noticed, not for the first time, were almost as pale as Kevin's. Rufus and his mother had green eyes. I liked the green better somehow" (90). The fact that Dana acknowledges a preference for Rufus's eye color suggests that she associates the paler color with the gaze of ownership that she has experienced with Tom Weylin. On some unconscious level, the gaze and color of the slave owner's eyes produce a connection with her husband. In another instance, Dana associates Kevin's physical expression of frustration with her memory of Tom Weylin. When Kevin returns to the present after spending a lengthy time in the nineteenth century, Dana tries to help him recover from the psychological traumas of living in the past for so long. When he pulls away from her and leaves the room in frustration, she notes: "The expression on his face was something I'd seen, something I was used to seeing on Tom Weylin. Something closed and ugly" (194). Much like the earlier associations she had made between the two men's eyes, Dana makes a connection between Tom and Kevin when she feels threatened. And like the comparisons Dana makes between slavery and apartheid, or between her life in poverty and the lives of the slaves on the Weylin plantation, Dana turns to the past in order to contextualize the present.

The comparisons that Dana makes between Rufus and Kevin extend beyond a physical resemblance and reflect a similarity in the ways the two men treat her as a woman. Both Kevin and Rufus demonstrate a desire to control and manipulate Dana by forcing her to perform tasks they are unwilling to perform themselves. In each instance, both men appeal to Dana's emotions in an attempt to convince her to act as their personal assistant. In the present, Kevin, a writer, wants her to type his manuscripts for him. In spite of the fact that Dana, herself, is a writer and avoids typing her own manuscripts, Kevin expects her to accommodate his needs before her own. His insistence that she perform this task produces a conflict between them that Dana continues to resent. This resentment manifests itself when Dana recalls the day Kevin proposed to her. As she narrates this important moment in their relationship, the memory of this conflict between them interrupts her account:

> He really had asked me to do some typing for him three times. I'd done it the first time, grudgingly, not telling him how much I hated typing. . . . That was why I was with a blue-collar agency instead of a white-collar agency. The second time he asked, though, I told him, and I refused. He was annoyed.

The third time when I refused again, he was angry. He said if I couldn't do
him a little favor when he asked, I could leave. So I went home. (109)

Though Dana and Kevin eventually reconcile the argument and get married, the fact that Dana recalls the incident while recounting his marriage
proposal suggests that it remains an unresolved issue and a source of conflict for her. A similar situation occurs in the past when Rufus asks Dana to
write letters for him. Facing the prospect of losing the plantation, Rufus
wants Dana to use her skills as a writer in an effort to hold off his debtors.
Dana grants his request in order to prevent him from selling more slaves
from his plantation. The fact that both men seek to benefit from Dana's
skills as a typist and a writer in spite of Dana's own desires indicates that
Kevin and Rufus place their own needs ahead of hers. Kevin's attitude
toward Dana in this regard represents a disturbing corollary to Rufus's
treatment of her in the past.

In addition to the similarities in the patriarchal attitudes both men
exhibit toward her, Dana herself demonstrates a protective tendency
toward both men. Even as she must concern herself with her own survival,
Dana wants to prevent the influences of the antebellum South from mark-
ing both Rufus and Kevin. When Dana realizes that she must play a critical role in Rufus's life, she looks upon that burden as an opportunity to
counteract the effects that slavery and white patriarchy will have on Rufus
as a young boy:

I thought of Rufus and his father, of Rufus becoming his father. It would
happen some day in at least one way. Someday Rufus would own the plantation. Someday he would be the slaveholder, responsible in his own right
for what happened to the people who lived in those half-hidden cabins.
The boy was literally growing up as I watched, growing up because I
watched and because I helped to keep him safe. I was the worst possible
guardian for him—a black to watch over him in a society that considered
blacks subhuman, a woman to watch over him in a society that considered
women perennial children, I would have all I could do to look after myself.
But I would help him as best I could. And I would try to keep the friendship with him, maybe plant a few ideas in his mind that would help me
and the people who would be his slaves in the years to come. I might even
be making things easier for Alice. (68)

As much as Dana wants to protect Rufus from the effects of slavery, her
primary desire is to change his attitudes and behavior toward the black

people on his plantation. However, for Rufus, the ideology of white, male superiority that perpetuated the slave system of the antebellum South proves too pervasive for him to overcome, even in his interactions with Dana. As he grows older, his desire to claim her as his property overrides his willingness to accept her as his equal.

Initially, Dana has a similar response to Kevin's experiences in the past. When he first travels back in time by holding her while she is transported, Dana realizes that he could remain stranded in the past if she were unable to bring him into the present with her. This prospect frightens her when she contemplates the effect the antebellum South may have on him. She states:

> A place like this could endanger him in a way that I didn't want to talk to him about. If he was stranded here for years, some part of this place could rub off on him. No large part, I knew. But if he survived here, it would be because he managed to tolerate the life here. He wouldn't have to take part in it, but he would have to keep quiet about it. Free speech and press hadn't done too well in the ante bellum South. Kevin wouldn't do too well either. The place, the time would either kill him outright or mark him somehow. I didn't like either possibility. (77–78)

Upon his initial encounter with the past, Kevin articulates his attraction toward the time period, giving voice to the fears Dana has kept to herself: "This would be a great time to live in. . . . I keep thinking what an experience it would be to stay in it—go West and watch the building of the country, see how much of the old West mythology is true" (77). When Dana responds that the West provided white people with an opportunity to exploit the Native Americans in the same way they exploited black people, she notes that his reaction is one of confused silence. In spite of the hardships Dana must endure in the past, the nineteenth century retains its romantic quality for Kevin. As Ashraf Rushdy notes, Kevin's tendency to demean Dana and her experiences in the past is an expanded version of his behavior toward her in their present life: "What Kevin's transportation to the past does is accentuate those residual aspects of his patriarchal thinking" ("Families" 149). Much like her concern that slavery will turn Rufus into a cruel and violent slave owner, Dana fears that the antebellum South would appeal to the baser aspects of Kevin's personality—aspects that she has witnessed even in their own relationship.

Eventually Dana's fear that Kevin could be stranded in the past becomes reality when Dana returns without him. As a result, Kevin must spend several months in nineteenth-century Maryland alone. During this time, Kevin maintains his integrity by leaving the Weylin plantation and participating in the anti-slavery movement, often helping slaves escape to the North. As his knowledge of the past increases, Kevin develops a greater ability to comprehend the impact slavery has on Dana. And yet, even toward the end of the novel, a gap still remains between Dana's perspective of the slave experience and his capacity to understand her response to the past. An example of this gap occurs when Dana tries to explain her complex relationship with Rufus. During one of her brief "trips" home, Kevin hesitantly asks Dana if Rufus has tried to rape her. Dana has a hard time conveying to him that she would kill Rufus or die before she would allow him to touch her in any way. She explains:

> I am not property, Kevin. I'm not a horse or a sack of wheat. If I have to seem to be property, if I have to accept the limits of my freedom for Rufus's sake, then he also has to accept limits—on his behavior toward me. He has to leave me enough control over my life to make living look better to me than killing or dying. (246)

Rather than an example of her strength of will, Dana feels that her reaction is a sign of her inability to endure all that violence that her ancestors endured in order to survive. Kevin responds by expressing his faith in her ability to withstand as much as her ancestors had. After their discussion, Dana feels as if Kevin understands her response to slavery better but admits that his faith in her "felt enough like truth for [her] not to mind that he only half understood" (246).

Though Kevin's ability to understand Dana improves as a result of his experiences in the past, Butler suggests that he can never completely identify with Dana's perspective of slavery. By leaving this gap unbridged, Butler suggests that Dana's and Kevin's experience of the past provides them with an impetus to deal with the complexities of their relationship that they had chosen to ignore in their brief courtship. By the end of the novel, both Dana and Kevin realize that their relationship cannot transcend the racism that persists as a legacy of slavery by simply isolating themselves from their relatives. Rather, they must confront its roots in the past and its impact on their present lives.

As complex and profound as the corollaries between Dana's interactions with Rufus and those with Kevin are, the most crucial and deeply rooted connection Dana must confront is the link between herself and her great-grandmother Alice Greenwood. Ultimately, the conflation of time that prompts the direct connections between these two women reflects the "authority of experience" that forms the foundation of Dana's (and Butler's) representation of the past. Although Rufus provides the impetus for Dana's time travel, I would argue that Dana's opportunity to understand her great-grandmother's hardships as a black woman in the nineteenth century constitutes the most challenging and potentially redemptive aspect of her confrontation with the past. As much as Dana must resolve her relationship with Kevin through her experiences with Rufus, she must also come to terms with her own place in the context of her heritage as the only remaining descendent of Alice. In the absence of a maternal figure in the present, Dana's confrontation with the past allows her to forge a bond with the primary maternal figure in the past. If Rufus represents "the patriarchal pull of the linear" that sends Dana into the past as critic Lucie Armitt suggests, then Alice represents the matriarchal pull of the *circular* that connects Dana's present identity with her spiritual and blood ancestor of the past. As an orphan, one alienated from her only living relatives, the conflation of time allows Dana to forge a connection to her past in order to ground herself in the present.

Initially, Dana's role as Rufus's protector and friend forces her to play an active part in Alice's sexual victimization and exploitation. As a result, her relationship with Alice is wrought with conflict and contradiction. Even as she befriends and identifies with Alice, Dana's commitment to saving Rufus's life ensures the fact that Alice will suffer at his hands. The clearest example of the impact this conflict has on Dana and Alice occurs when Dana prevents Alice's husband, Isaac, from killing Rufus for making sexual advances toward his wife. Even though she helps Alice and Isaac escape the plantation, by allowing Rufus to survive, Dana allows him to pursue the two of them in their attempt to escape slavery. As punishment for running away and in revenge for his relationship with Alice, Rufus has Isaac's ears cut off and sells him to a Mississippi trader. When Rufus returns to the plantation with Alice, who is badly injured and unconscious, Dana nurses her back to health. Once Alice recovers from her injuries, she confronts Dana about her role in the events that led to her capture:

"If you had any sense, you would have let him die!"

"If I had, it wouldn't have kept you and Isaac from being caught. It might have gotten you both killed though if anyone had guessed what Isaac had done."

"Doctor-nigger," she said with contempt. "Think you know so much. Reading-nigger. *White-nigger!* Why didn't you know enough to let me die?" (160)

Alice's despair at being reclaimed by Rufus as his property induces her to lash out at Dana in a manner that, she feels, will hurt her most deeply. Dana endures her rebukes because she realizes that Alice has no one else toward whom she can vent her anger and because she senses her own culpability in Alice's suffering. Though Dana feels that preventing Rufus's death was in Alice's and Isaac's best interest, she cannot escape the fact that her decision also ensured the continuation of her family line.[10]

As Dana spends more time in the past, she begins to concern herself less with perpetuating her family line and more with the survival of the other slaves on the plantation. Part of Dana's process of understanding the connections between herself and Alice lies in her realization that she cannot exist in the past as an outsider. As her experience of slavery deepens and her relationships with the other slaves grow, Dana can no longer separate her twentieth-century identity from the ways it has been marked by the past. As Sandra Govan points out, in spite of the differences between Dana as a free, educated twentieth-century woman and Alice as a nineteenth-century woman forced into the ignorance and passivity of slavery, Butler establishes a link between them that grows the longer Dana spends in the past (93). Rather than merely playing the role of observer, Dana finds that her life in the antebellum South has changed her on a deeply psychological level. As she tends to her duties on the plantation late in the novel, Dana realizes that, in essence, she has become a slave, mentally and physically:

> I turned and went back out of the house, out toward the woods. I had to think. I wasn't getting enough time to myself. Once—God knows how long ago—I had worried that I was keeping too much distance between myself and this alien time. Now, there was no distance at all. When had I stopped acting? Why had I stopped? (221)

Though this realization illustrates the extent to which slavery has interpellated Dana into its system of subjugation and oppression, it also represents the beginning of Dana's ability to forge a closer bond with Alice. Once Dana fully comprehends the bonds that link her with Alice, her grandmother Hagar is born. Dana ensures the continuance of her family line both by saving Rufus's life and by establishing a relationship with Alice, her spiritual and blood ancestor.

The bond that Dana builds with Alice is as complex as the one she forges with Rufus. On one level, Alice represents a maternal presence in Dana's life—the ancestral figure that gave birth to her existence in the twentieth century. In this sense, the conflation of time gives Dana the opportunity to experience the mother-daughter relationship she has been denied by the death of her parents. Dana's time travel allows her to play a maternal role to her own ancestor. In this context, Dana acts as Alice's confidante as she tries to protect her from Rufus's destructive sexual desires. Ironically, Rufus, as the man who compels them to forge a union in mutual resistance, characterizes their bond most clearly when he tells them, "You are really one woman. Did you know that?" (228). Though Rufus's observation reflects his inability to see them as individual women outside of his desire to claim ownership of them, Dana and Alice acknowledge their uncanny physical resemblance as a result of this statement. Unlike the faint traces of resemblance between Kevin and Tom Weylin, the physical similarities between Dana and Alice, in addition to the experiences they share as black women, reflect their bond as spiritual and blood relatives. For Rufus, Dana and Alice are incomplete halves of one whole. But for Dana, the conflation of time establishes the connections between her life in the present and her ancestor's life in the past as part of one continuous existence.

In her final encounter with the past, Dana learns that Alice has killed herself after Rufus threatens to sell her children. With her death, Rufus turns to Dana as a substitute for Alice, once again conflating the two women as "two halves of a whole" (257). For Rufus, Dana represents another opportunity to possess and dominate Alice. As he begins to rape her, Dana stabs him, resisting his claim of ownership over her much like Alice refused to submit to a life of slavery. As they struggle with one another, Rufus grabs Dana's arm the moment she is transported to the present. As a result, Dana loses her arm, retaining a permanent mark of the past on the contours of her body. For Ashraf Rushdy, the loss of Dana's arm represents "a symptom of how recovering the past involves losing a grip on the present" ("Families" 139). In other words, her physical loss illustrates the price one pays for engaging the past. But the trauma of losing her limb during her final act of resistance to slavery also symbolizes the extent to which the past scars us even in the present. In essence, slavery affects Dana's life in the present on both physical and psychological terms. She must endure the legacy of slavery not only through her memories of her past experiences but also through its physical manifestations that persist even in her present life.

Dana's confrontation with the past allows her to gain a deeper understanding of slavery and the horrors her ancestors had to endure at the hands of those who perpetuated this particular system of oppression. But, perhaps even more important, the conflation of time gives Dana access to knowledge of the past that extends beyond the limited historical accounts that document slavery as an institution. In the epilogue, Dana describes her adjustment to life in the present and her slow process of recovering from her experiences in the past. In order to come to terms with all that she has seen, she and Kevin return to present-day Maryland in order to conduct research on the Weylin plantation after her final visit. From the official historical record, Dana learns that the house was destroyed in a fire on the day of her last encounter and that most of the slaves had been sold in order to pay for the damages. Although there is information on Rufus's death and his mother's departure from the plantation, there are no detailed records of the slaves and their lives. As a result, Dana's experiences in the past and her narrative account of them stand as the only record of Alice's life and the birth of her grandmother Hagar. As such, the conflation of time allows Dana to bridge the gap between the official accounts of slavery and the lived experiences of her ancestors. Perhaps it was the gap itself that produced the impetus for Dana's time travel in the first place. By providing an account of her ancestors who have been obscured by the historical record, Dana no longer needs to return to the past as a means of understanding the slave experience from the slaves' perspective.

In many ways Dana Franklin is the fictional counterpart to Octavia Butler herself: a contemporary woman faced with the difficult task of coming to terms with the history of slavery. Butler's novel dramatizes both Dana's and her own attempts to achieve narrative authority over the past. Time travel in *Kindred,* much like the material anachronisms in *Flight to Canada,* reflects the contemporary black writer's reliance on the "authority of experience" even across time and space. In their re-formation of the past, non-mimetic conventions provide Reed and Butler with the narrative flexibility to connect subjectivities separated by over a century. This is a narrative conceit that undermines the basic foundations of historical realism and reinscribes a faith in the stability of racial (and communal) identity across time and space. Such a gesture rejects postmodern conceptions of race and identity even as it relies on the deconstructive aspects of postmodern history. Butler's novel, even more than Reed's, straddles the line between the identity politics of black nationalism and black feminism and the anti-foundationalism of postmodern thought.

GHOSTS, HAUNTED HOUSES, AND
THE LEGACY OF SLAVERY

TONI MORRISON'S *BELOVED* AND THE GOTHIC IMPULSE

T HE traces of non-mimetic genres like science fiction and the post-modern novel in postmodern slave narratives serve to hybridize an already hybrid narrative form. The original slave narratives, drawing as they did from the sentimental novel, spiritual autobiographies, captivity narratives, and abolitionist political tracts, combined elements of these diverse and, in some cases, popular genres in order to address the issue of slavery on multiple ideological levels. As we have seen in *Kindred* and *Flight to Canada,* postmodern slave narratives reflect the influence not only of these nineteenth-century forms but also of twentieth-century popular and non-mimetic forms that ultimately expand the narrative canvas and open their texts up to aesthetically liberating representations of slavery. However, the increased hybridity of these texts results not in a preoccupation with formal technique or parodic self-referentiality characteristic of postmodern novels but in a repoliticization of the narrative forms of which it is composed. Rather than relying on more contemporary genres, Toni Morrison's postmodern slave narrative, *Beloved,* turns to the gothic novel, a popular eighteenth- and nineteenth-century narrative genre, as a means of re-forming the past. Much as Reed and Butler did with contemporary literary forms, Morrison invokes the gothic novel in order to expand the parameters of the original slave narrative and traditional history. In the process she invests the gothic novel, a largely stylized and apolitical genre in its original form, with overtly historical and political dimensions.

As most critics agree, the gothic novel developed in Europe in the late eighteenth century amidst the tension between Enlightenment rationalism and the aesthetics of the sublime: the region of art and the metaphysical world beyond reason and science. As Fred Botting points out, in its earliest incarnation, the gothic was both revered and criticized as a literature of transgression and excess—a popular presentation of "supernatural, sensational and terrifying incidents [that] . . . produced emotional effects on its readers rather than developing a rational or properly cultivated response" (5). As the gothic narrative developed in the nineteenth and twentieth century and ingrained itself in the American literary imagination through writers like Charles Brockden Brown and Edgar Allan Poe, the form expanded beyond the haunted castles and disturbing terrain of the American landscape to include the darker aspects of the self and madness. The persistence of the gothic in the contemporary imagination manifests itself in varied and multiple ways as successful films like *The Sixth Sense* (2001) and *The Others* (2002) illustrate. However, even in its earliest and original form, the gothic's evocative symbolic dimensions—its ability to represent the repressed individual unconscious, the cultural anxieties of an increasingly complex social world, or even the abstract nature of evil—perhaps explain its continued presence in twenty-first-century texts. As Allan Lloyd Smith suggests, the gothic as a cultural form shares key elements with postmodernism ranging from an emphasis on narrative indeterminacy to elements of parody and pastiche. Smith argues that both "confront the embattled, deconstructed self, without sureties of religion and social place, or any coherent psychology observed in both the Enlightenment or modernist traditions" (7). But where the gothic and postmodernism represent the past "without discrimination, as a fancy dress worn by contemporary sensibility" (10), Morrison confronts the history of slavery with an ideological purpose grounded in liberating the past from discourses like the gothic and postmodernism.

In turning to the gothic novel, Morrison establishes her postmodern slave narrative in opposition not only to the truth claims of realism and objectivity of traditional history but to the ways the form itself contributes to our tendency to abstract and aestheticize the history of slavery. For Morrison (and other writers of postmodern slave narratives), slavery and its legacy are real, historical examples of systematized oppression that finds its expression (and its perpetuation) in the literary forms that depict it. Where traditional narrative history, in its claims of objectivity and realism, obscures the lives and struggles of those who endured slavery, the gothic dimensions of nineteenth-century representations of slavery (ranging from the slave narratives themselves to popular novels like *Uncle Tom's Cabin*) abstract, fetishize, and obscure the real conditions of slavery though a stylized and conventionalized literary form.[1] Traditional historical and fictional narratives that use gothic elements not only fail to address the history of slavery in liberating terms but also undermine the process of liberation by drawing on the pleasures associated with that popular form. In *Beloved,* Morrison creates an alternative representation of slavery that mines the formal dimensions of the gothic novel but forces readers to shift their focus away from the fantastic elements like the haunted house and the ghost toward the "real" gothic elements of the text: slavery itself and those who systematically perpetuated it. Morrison has stated that one purpose of the gothic elements in the novel "is to keep the reader preoccupied with the nature of the incredible spirit world while being supplied with a controlled diet of the incredible political world" ("Unspeakable" 32). As this statement suggests, Morrison deploys the gothic as a strategy to illustrate both worlds are equally incredible and, in many ways, connected. Each impulse—one toward politics, the other toward the aesthetic representation of evil—plays off the other in the novel and forces readers to reconceptualize the presence of gothic elements in her text and as a narrative form intimately linked to the discourse on slavery.

Morrison's manipulation of gothic conventions reveals a particular orientation toward the form as a whole. More than merely a literary genre, the gothic is a discourse unto itself—a way of viewing and representing the world. In its rich symbolism of creaky doors, hidden passageways, spectral figures, the gothic is marked by its own ideology, sometimes easily visible, and others, shadowy and elusive. As Fredric Jameson argues, the production of any aesthetic form "is an ideological act in its own right, with the function of inventing imaginary or formal 'solutions' to unresolvable social contradictions" (*Political* 79). Clearly the gothic, particularly its prevalence in nineteenth-century American literature, reflects an attempt to resolve the contradictions of slavery and the African presence in the American landscape. In fact, this is Morrison's own view of the American literary tradition. In her monograph *Playing in the Dark,* Morrison discusses her view of the American form of the romance as a fundamentally historical form. Her statements apply equally well to the gothic. She writes:

> Romance, an exploration of anxiety imported from the shadows of European culture, made possible the sometimes safe and other times risky embrace of quite specific, understandably human, fears: Americans' fear of being outcast, of failing, of powerlessness. . . . Romance offered writers not

less but more; not a narrow a-historical canvas but a wide historical one; not escape but entanglement . . . (and) the opportunity to conquer fear imaginatively and to quiet deep insecurities. It offered platforms for moralizing and fabulation, and for the imaginative entertainment of violence, sublime incredibility, and terror—and terror's most significant, overweening ingredient: darkness, with all the connotative value it awakened. (36–37)

Morrison suggests that the gothic has as its silent underpinning the real historical landscape of the American frontier and the legacy of slavery. As such, the gothic impulse intersects with the political and historical reality of slavery and derives its force from the anxieties that such a systemized form of exploitation and degradation produces. In other words, the desire to obscure and abstract violence through the gothic itself has its political and ideological source in the social condition of slavery.

Toni Morrison's orientation toward the gothic forces us to shift our analysis from the traditional gothic elements of the text to the complex aesthetic, historical, philosophical, and interpretive systems that link the form with American slavery. As a result, *Beloved* resists conventional interpretive strategies associated with the genre. Although Morrison uses highly symbolic elements reminiscent of gothic novels such as ghosts, haunted houses, violence, and ambiguity, her treatment of these tropes within the specific historical context of American slavery challenges us to confront them in simultaneously concrete yet open-ended ways. On one hand, Morrison forces readers to accept the ambiguous and supernatural qualities associated with gothic elements like the haunting of the house at 124 Bluestone Road or the presence of the ghost in corporeal form. Much like instances of magical realism, both the readers and the characters accept these fantastic occurrences as part of the literary landscape. However, Morrison simultaneously reinvests the realistic dimensions of her text— the sexual and violent brutality of slavery—with elements of gothic ambiguity and open-endedness. What becomes "gothic" in Morrison's novel is not the presence of the supernatural but the very real, very human aspects of slavery. As a result, we as readers ultimately must reject traditional interpretations of gothic symbolism if we want to avoid perpetuating the abstract and aestheticized representations of slavery that Morrison implicitly critiques in her novel.

Psychoanalytic readings of the gothic represent one interpretive strategy that emphasizes symbolic and abstract dimensions of the gothic form. Based largely on Freud's view of the gothic as the "return of the repressed" in his essay "The Uncanny," psychoanalytic readings often dehistoricize the gothic as a convention and regard its presence as a universal expression harkening back to castration complexes and childhood anxieties and fears. Like a dream, the gothic elements of a text become pure objects for interpretation, pregnant symbols of limitless potential meaning rooted in an individual's identity formation. Although more recent psychoanalytic readings of the gothic reject the explicit phallocentrism of Freud's reading, they often obscure its historical dimensions even further. Julia Kristeva's view of the gothic impulse, which she calls the "abject," represents "not even the shadow of a memory" and is "above all ambiguity" (7–9). For Kristeva the impulse toward the gothic pre-exists even the unconscious or the oedipal complex and resides in the realm of the pre-conscious and universal. Under this interpretive rubric, the gothic text is always in the process of becoming, its metaphorical feet never firmly touching the ground. Psychoanalytic models of interpretation serve the abstract quality of the narrative, dehistoricizing it and linking it to "the problematic of the individual subject and the individual psychobiography" (Jameson, *The Political Unconscious* 66). *Beloved*, although certainly rich in psychological complexity, is also deeply rooted in the context of American slavery, its symbolism grounded in a moment of history that resonates into the present.

Any reading of the gothic elements in *Beloved* must account for its emphasis on history rather than merely the hidden unconscious of the individual. At the same time, it also seems necessary to acknowledge this historical context as the articulated *foundation* of the gothic impulse rather than as an encoded and allegorical subtext. Whereas more recent theories of the gothic like Vijay Mishra's *The Gothic Sublime* view the form as "a symbolic structure, historically determined . . . by capitalism" which "tropes the sublime as the unthinkable, the unnamable, and the unspeakable," Morrison's novel seeks to speak the history and draw a direct link between the violence and horror of slavery and its gothic narrative expression (23).[2] The historical basis for these narratives' exploration of the violence of slavery stands in the foreground of the text rather than as a hidden symbolic structure manifesting itself in the gothic impulse. As a result, historical interpretations that see the gothic as a metaphor for actual historical events and the expression of a culture's sublimated anxieties of political uncertainty, even when grounded in the specificities of capitalism, remain inadequate when applying them to Toni Morrison's re-formation of the gothic which articulates history directly into the text.

Where does this leave us, then, in terms of analyzing Morrison's use of the gothic in *Beloved*, if the novel resists both psychoanalytic interpretation and, for the most part, the uncovering of a hidden historical subtext? Clearly Morrison's novel insists on the reader's active interpretation of the complicated and ambiguous elements in her text. I would argue that the gothic conventions in *Beloved* resist an "encoding-decoding" model of interpretation in favor of a process of reading engaged in the simultaneous reconstruction of history and the reflexive critique of previous attempts to obscure and silence specific histories. In other words, any reading of the gothic dimensions in *Beloved* must take into account Morrison's implicit commentary on the gothic as both an aesthetic and an ideological discourse. It is not that *Beloved* rejects all interpretive strategies as much as it deploys them still intact within a context that must, necessarily, resist their abstracting qualities.

My reading of *Beloved* as a re-formation of the gothic novel and the slave narrative draws on two central and related aspects of the novel: Beloved's presence as a character in the text and the concept of "rememory." Rather than focusing on these two components as physical manifestations of Sethe's repressed memories or as elements of magical realism, Morrison's characterization of Beloved and her treatment of rememory work in tandem to emphasize the inherent complexities of representing the history of slavery in either realistic or gothic terms. More than merely gothic elements of the text, Beloved and rememory function as symbolic markers or signifiers of an oppositional historiography that combine elements of historical realism and the fantastic. On one hand, the gothic figure of Beloved as a ghost represents the open-ended and highly ambiguous dimensions of the past. As a character and a symbol, she occupies multiple spaces and holds multiple meanings. As the other characters in the novel try to interpret her presence in the material world, they ultimately must come to terms with the fact that she resists any single or coherent definition. By infusing Beloved with complex and ambiguous dimensions, Morrison retains traditional elements of the gothic but prevents us from understanding her through any one interpretive thread. She stands as a sliding and almost incoherent signifier of slavery—one that resists narrative stability. In contrast, the concept of rememory asserts the ability of the past to maintain its surface traces in the physical world of the present. Although Beloved remains elusive to those who would contain her, the concept of rememory suggests that we have access to the past through its physical re-emergence in the present. As Sethe defines it, rememories can lie in the places where history has occurred, in the houses and trees that have witnessed slavery. By juxtaposing the open-ended dimensions of the past (Beloved) with its material traces in the present (rememory),

Morrison maintains a conception of historicity and creates a text that resists the abstraction of violence in the gothic and the limitations of traditional narrative history.

The fact that Morrison confronts slavery through such a complex narrative strategy suggests that her novel resists facile classification either as a historical fiction or as a purely imaginative text. As Paul Gilroy points out, Morrison, and other contemporary writers who address the history of slavery, exhibits "a degree of discomfort with the novel [form] and a shared anxiety about its utility as a resource in the social processes that govern the remaking and conservation of historical memory" (218–19). In the face of this anxiety, Morrison expands the form of the gothic novel in order to address the complexity of slavery, creating both a historical fiction and a fictional history. The shifting narrative structure and infusion of elements of the fantastic have led some critics to regard *Beloved* as a modernist text. Linda Krumholz argues that Morrison "adapts techniques from modernist novels, such as the fragmentation of the plot and a shifting narrative voice, to compel the reader to actively construct an interpretive framework" (376). Conversely, Rafael Perez-Torres points to the same qualities to argue that Morrison "deploys a narrative pastiche" characteristic of postmodern novels "in order to contest history as a master narrative" (194). The fact that Morrison's approach to fictionalizing history can appear as both modernist and postmodernist suggests that the novel itself, much like the character for which it is named, cannot be pinned down. Whether modern or postmodern, historical or imaginative, *Beloved* directs itself toward the active reader, encouraging us to interpret not only the events of the narrative but also cultural discourses that inform the ways those events are structured in narrative. Morrison fuses form and content, aesthetics and politics, modernist and postmodernist devices, and, perhaps most significantly, history and fiction in such a way that we must engage the novel on its own terms and within its own structures. The primary components of the novel, the uncanny quality of Beloved's appearance in the text and rememory, become avenues into interpreting Morrison's oppositional conception of narrative history.

The haunted house and Beloved, herself, constitute the initial arena for Morrison's transformation of the gothic. From the outset of the novel, Morrison invokes the gothic form by proclaiming the spitefulness of 124 and by detailing the effect this haunted house has had on those who have lived there. Although Sethe and Denver (and Baby Suggs when she was alive) accept and even welcome the presence of the ghost, Sethe's sons, Howard and Buglar, leave because of the supernatural events that plague the household. As Carol Schmudde points out, Morrison establishes 124 Bluestone Road as "both the traditional haunted house of the conventional ghost story, and a radically possessed and repossessed arena of historic and mythic confrontation" (409–10). In addition to history and myth, Morrison also uses the haunted house as the site for an aesthetic confrontation of the gothic form. Early in the novel, Morrison transforms the traditional ghost story by establishing Beloved's actual physical appearance after Paul D has exorcized the ghost from the house. Beloved's emergence from the water, fully dressed and smiling, signals a shift away from a spectral haunting to a concrete confrontation with the history of slavery and its effects. Instead of an abstract, invisible force that wreaks havoc on the unsuspecting inhabitants of the house, Beloved assumes the role of a character in the text, one whose presence all the other characters accept as real. Her conversion from spirit to corporeal form disentangles Beloved from traditional aspects of the uncanny associated with the gothic.

Initially Beloved's presence in the text provides the reader with material for a psychoanalytic interpretation. Although Sethe herself resists this explanation of her existence at first, we immediately suspect Beloved is the incarnation of the ghost and the return of Sethe's daughter. Morrison encourages this interpretation by linking the two women symbiotically. Beloved feeds off Sethe's mind and body from the moment of her emergence into the real world. When Sethe encounters Beloved on the road back from the carnival, she experiences an intense physical reaction she cannot explain. As Beloved drinks cup after cup of water, Sethe's body purges as if her water has broken in the act of giving birth:

> Not since she was a baby girl . . . had she had an emergency that unmanageable. She never made the outhouse. Right in front of its door she had to lift her skirts, and the water she voided was endless. . . . She tidied herself and ran around to the porch. No one was there. All three were inside— Paul D and Denver standing before the stranger, watching her drink cup after cup of water. (51)

As the novel progresses, both Sethe and the reader come to accept Beloved's presence as the physical manifestation of the daughter she has killed, brought into existence by Sethe's unrelenting efforts to beat back the past. Beloved is, in literal terms, the return of the repressed. Once she begins to see Beloved as the specter of the past, Sethe seems to shrink physically as Beloved grows and becomes more radiant. In essence, Sethe's acceptance of a psychological interpretation of Beloved's gothic presence works in tandem with Beloved's destructive consumption of her. For Sethe, this interpretation leads to her continuing descent into the mystifying forces Beloved unleashes upon her. For the reader, such an interpretation is equally problematic; it not only constrains Beloved as a symbol of slavery, it renders her presence abstract and gothic. However, Beloved's physicality resists a psychoanalytic interpretation. Although Morrison evokes the constructs of Freudian psychology as much as the gothic form itself through Beloved, it is an uneven fit in need of re-formation.[3]

More than just a product of Sethe's individual need to repress the past, Beloved also seems to encourage interpretation as a product of a collective or cultural unconscious by playing a significant role in the lives of the other characters in the novel. Denver initially sees in Beloved a connection to her past that her mother never articulates—the lost sister that quells the solitude and provides a connection to the outside world. Paul D, at first, experiences Beloved as a way to express the emotions he has locked away from himself. In this sense Beloved could stand as the manifestation of a communal unconscious—the symbol of a slave past submerged and forgotten by the black community. Ultimately, however, Beloved's presence in the text stands as a concrete illustration of the horrors of slavery consuming the present. For Denver, Paul D, and even the community as a whole, Beloved represents both a real present/presence and the horrific possibility of the past rearing its ugly head.

Toni Morrison further suggests a movement away from an interpretive strategy that focuses on Beloved as the product of the unconscious, collective or individual, by endowing the character with her own consciousness and a possible historic past. Morrison gives Beloved's consciousness full expression late in the novel; she allows Beloved a narrative voice—a kind of ghost speech which conveys elements of the slave past.[4] Morrison also offers the possibility that Beloved has a "real" history when Stamp Paid suggests that she is the same girl who has recently escaped repeated sexual and physical abuse at the hands of a white man and his son. These, however, are merely possibilities that do little to explain the obvious symbiotic connections between Beloved and Sethe that Morrison's text encourages. In fact, Morrison seems to render any objective and rational explanation of Beloved's existence as unsatisfying as a psychological one. Beloved is neither an abstraction nor a real person. Beloved defies interpretation. Beloved *is*.

As much as Beloved represents the ghost of Sethe's daughter, she also symbolizes the aspect of history (or more specifically, the history of slavery) that can never be explained or catalogued. As a character, a signifier, and a symbol, she threatens incomprehensibility even after Paul D drives her ghost from 124 Bluestone Road and forces her to emerge in physical form. Beloved exists in a state of perpetual liminality, caught between slavery and the present moment of social (and narrative) reconstruction, between the spirit and material world, between the real and the imaginary. As such, she risks losing stable form and content for herself, the characters in the novel, and perhaps even the reader. Beloved's simultaneously symbolic and literal lack of cohesion becomes apparent when she contemplates a tooth she has pulled from her mouth:

> Beloved looked at the tooth and thought, This is it. Next would be her arm, her hand, a toe. Pieces of her would drop maybe one at a time, maybe all at once. Or on one of those mornings before Denver woke and after Sethe left she would fly apart. It is difficult keeping her head on her neck, her legs attached to her hips when she is by herself. Among the things she could not remember was when she first knew that she could wake up any day and find herself in pieces. She had two dreams: exploding, and being swallowed. When her tooth came out—an odd fragment, last in the row—she thought it was starting. (133)

Morrison's construction of Beloved as both a character and a sign of slavery itself encourages us to read this passage literally and figuratively. In literal terms, Beloved, in the present, retains the fragmentary quality of her ghostly form. Even as she exists in the material world, her body threatens to disperse and lose coherence. In figurative and even post-structuralist terms, the multiple meanings the other characters assign to Beloved threaten to overwhelm and swallow her. As a symbol or sign of the "sixty million or more" lost in the Middle Passage, Beloved cannot hope to maintain singularity or coherence. For Sethe, she is the daughter who has returned from the dead to offer redemption for her sins. For Denver, she is the sister who rescues her from the solitude of 124. For Paul D, she is the child-woman who exposes the "red heart" he has hidden away from the pain of the past. For the other characters in the community, she represents the remnants of a past they would forget and the loved ones that they lost to the horrors of slavery.

Nowhere is Beloved's expansiveness more apparent than in the poetic monologues toward the end of the novel. In these brief vignettes, Morrison portrays the streams of consciousness of her three protagonists: Sethe, Denver, and Beloved. In each monologue, one of the women attempts to define Beloved's meaning and the implications of her existence in the material world. In Beloved's narrative, Morrison conveys the elusiveness of her identity as symbol and character by constructing her speech without punctuation or logical grammatical structure. Beloved mixes tenses, speaking from the past and the present simultaneously, crossing the boundaries of the spiritual and the physical, speaking of the interconnections between women trapped by slavery:

> I am Beloved and she is mine. . . . how can I say things that are pictures I
> am not separate from her there is no place where I stop her face is my own
> and I want to be there in the place where her face is and to be looking at it
> too a hot thing All of it is now it is always now. (210)

Beloved exists in a state where language cannot convey meaning. She cannot separate her individual identity from all those identities that surround her. Representing both the horrors of the middle passage in which countless Africans perished and the qualities that mark her as Sethe's murdered daughter, Beloved's voice is fragmentary yet vast in scope.

As a result of the ambiguity and almost incomprehensibility of her existence as a character and symbol, Beloved contains a meaning that corresponds to the equally incomprehensible violence and exploitation rendered under American slavery. Although Beloved cannot be understood by coherent and conventional interpretive strategies, the major characters of the text eventually come to terms with her multiplicity of meaning. Ultimately, Denver is the character that best comprehends Beloved's existence in spite of her elusiveness. As Ashraf Rushdy argues in his essay "Daughters Signifyin(g) History," Denver emerges as the true daughter of history based on her ability to make sense of Beloved's existence in the material world and the pain of slavery that she symbolizes. What Denver represents in the novel is "the space for hearing the tale of infanticide with a degree of understanding" that allows her "to perform a healing narrative" (586). When Paul D sees Denver in the street after Beloved has been excised from the material world, he asks her whether she thinks Beloved was her sister returned from the dead. Denver replies: "At times. At times I think she was—more" (266). The ambiguity surrounding Beloved's meaning ultimately results not in empty signification, but in the expansiveness of meaning necessary in coming to terms with slavery. Rather than relegating slavery to the closure of traditional historical discourse or the fetishized aesthetics of the gothic, Morrison creates Beloved as a symbol of the "sixty million and more" of those who had suffered through slavery.

Although Morrison's construction of Beloved foregrounds our inability to comprehend fully this aspect of our past, she refuses to allow her narrative representation of slavery to remain in a state of historical ambiguity and indeterminacy. Morrison counteracts Beloved's esoteric qualities through her concept of "rememory." Rememory in the novel renders the abstract, psychologized past a concrete, physical reality. Rather than the return of an individual or collective unconscious, Beloved as the product of rememory is the physical presence of the past in the present.

To assert that rememory functions as the organizing force of *Beloved* is perhaps to state the obvious. Several critics have focused on varying aspects of the concept and the impact it has on the narrative itself. Mae Henderson argues that rememory represents the residual images of Sethe's past that she must transform "into a historical discourse shaped by narrativity" (66). Rememories mark the return, in physical form, of Sethe's repressed past to which she must give meaning through narrative. For Linda Krumholz, rememory allows Morrison to construct "a parallel between the individual processes of psychological recovery and a historical or national process" (395). Krumholz argues that rememory is the symbolic representation of a "historical unconscious" that forces the reader into a confrontation with the history of slavery much in the same way Sethe must come to terms with her past. Each of these interpretations accentuates the balance between the psychological and the historical dimensions of slavery—a balance noticeably and tragically absent from the official history of American slavery. However, rememory also allows Morrison to combine elements of historical realism, gothic fantasy, and narrative authority by asserting the past's physical traces in the present. Beyond its function as a *textual* element, the concept of rememory establishes both the materiality and the gothic aspects implicit in the history and historiography of slavery. Whereas Beloved derives her meaning from her expansiveness as a symbol or signifier of slavery, rememory opens the door to the more stable and grounded aspects of the past. As a result, Morrison's text achieves both the authority of "realistic" historical fiction and the narrative free play so essential to a liberating re-formation of the past.

Defined early in the novel by Sethe, rememory offers the reader the most lucid explanation for Beloved's appearance at 124 Bluestone Road and provides us with a conception of past and present that renders the history of slavery as real and accessible even to those who have never experienced it. In a conversation with her daughter Denver, Sethe warns her of the past's perpetual hold on the present:

"Some things go. Pass on. Some things just stay. I used to think it was my rememory. You know. Some things you forget. Other things you never do. But it's not. Places, places are still there. If a house burns down, it's gone—but the place—the picture of it—stays, and not just in my rememory, but out there in the world. What I remember is a picture floating around out there outside my head. I mean, even if I don't think it, even if I die, the picture of what I did, or knew, or saw is still out there. Right in the place where it happened."

"Can other people see it?" asked Denver.

"Oh yes. Oh yes, yes, yes. Someday you be walking down the road and you hear something or see something going on. So clear. And you think it's you thinking it up. A thought picture. But no. It's when you bump into a rememory that belongs to somebody else. Where I was before I came here, that place is real. It's never going away. Even if the whole farm—every tree and blade of grass of it dies. The picture is still there and what's more, if you go there—you who was never there—if you go there and stand in the place where it was, it will happen again; it will be there for you, waiting for you. So, Denver, you can't never go there. Never. Because even though it's all over—over and done with—it's going to always be there waiting for you." (35–36)

As Sethe conceptualizes it, rememory is the aspect of the past that exists apart from her own internal consciousness and exerts itself in the material present. Although connected to her individual memories (in the form of thought pictures), rememories have their own agency in the real world, converting abstract and formless thought into material reality. Sethe asserts that places (Sweet Home plantation), people (Beloved's ghost), and even nature itself (the trees and grass) contain the text of slavery on its surfaces as readable markers of the past. Within the context of the novel, rememory evokes both the supernatural in its suggestion that the past can haunt the present in physical form and traditional historicism in its conception of the past as an accessible and knowable reality.

Morrison's inclusion of rememory as a central concept of the novel allows her to convert Beloved from an unstable and incoherent signifier of slavery into a surface trace of the past in the present. Seen as the product of Sethe's rememory, Beloved, as both a signifier and a character, begins to achieve coherence and singularity. She is not the material manifestation of Sethe's unconscious as much as she is the physical remnant of slavery exerting itself into the present. For Sethe (and for readers as well), Beloved stands as the reincarnation of Sethe's daughter and the materiality of the history of slavery as well. In these terms, Beloved, no longer a sliding signifier, achieves stable content and meaning as a specific (and real) marker of Sethe's past. She is both the signifier and the signified. Engaging rememory as a concept forces us as readers to acknowledge Beloved's status as both elusive and concrete within the text. She is Denver's sister returned from the dead, but she is also, at times, much more.

As much as rememory represents a perpetual danger to Sethe, Denver, and other characters in the text, it also allows them to confront the violence that continues to rupture their present lives. Because rememory renders the past as a material reality, slavery becomes a text that resists abstraction through a process of narrativity. Beloved's re-emergence in physical form gives Sethe the opportunity to read the surface traces of her past and to convert them into a coherent form. Rememory grants her the authority to tell the story of Beloved's death on the basis of her ability to interpret the event she had been previously unable to confront. Even Denver can claim the authority to narrate the past although she herself has never experienced it. Beloved's materiality allows her to gain an intimate understanding of slavery and its impact on her mother's life. Morrison's concept of rememory and her characterization of Beloved allow her to posit an alternative historiography that can claim the best of both worlds: the claims of truth and coherence evidenced in traditional history and the ambiguity and expansiveness of non-mimetic forms like the gothic. *Beloved* achieves narrative authority over the past by both asserting slavery's elusiveness and gothic dimensions as a historical reality and conceptualizing the past as a knowable component of the present. Far from rejecting the gothic as a useful narrative tool for addressing the past, Morrison deploys the form to address the real, though disturbing and inexplicable, aspects of slavery. The presence of the gothic allows Morrison to relocate questions regarding the nature of evil from the supernatural realm to the systems of meaning that form the foundation of American slavery as an institution.

Just as the interaction between Beloved and rememory renders the abstract gothic concrete, the presence of schoolteacher, the representation of Enlightenment thinking and traditional history in the text, renders the "rational" gothic.[5] Schoolteacher, the overseer of the Sweet Home plantation and the man directly responsible for Sethe's most brutal memories of slavery, subjects her and the other slaves to the objectifying gaze of "scientific" or rational discourse. Even as he whips Sethe's back into a "chokecherry tree" and allows his nephews to "steal" her milk, schoolteacher's primary method of subjugation is his attempt to contain and dehumanize her through the control of knowledge and meaning.[6] Sethe recalls overhearing schoolteacher instructing his students on the proper classification of slaves:

> I couldn't help listening to what I heard that day. He was talking to his pupils and I heard him say, "Which one are you doing?" And one of the boys say, "Sethe." That's when I stopped because I heard my name, and then I took a few steps to where I could see what they was doing. Schoolteacher was standing over one of them with one hand behind his back. He licked a forefinger a couple of times and turned a few pages. Slow. I was about to turn around and keep on my way to where the muslin was, when I heard him say, "No, no. That's not the way. I told you to put her human characteristics on the left; her animal ones on the right. And don't forget to line them up." (193)

Schoolteacher's emphasis on a detached and "scientific" representation of Sethe relegates her humanity to a list of written qualities. For Mae Henderson, in "Toni Morrison's *Beloved*," schoolteacher, as "a data collector, cataloger, classifier, and taxonomist concerned with matters of materiality and empiricism," functions as a representation of traditional Western historiography, by dividing and dismembering the "indivisibility of the slave's humanity to reconstruct [or perhaps deconstruct] the slave in his text" (70). His analysis restricts any acknowledgment of Sethe's internal consciousness, a stance in direct contrast to the subject of the novel as a whole. Morrison contrasts the ordered quality of schoolteacher's list with the disordered and potentially incomprehensible nature of Beloved as both symbol and character. As Karla Holloway notes, "the 'ghostly'/'historical' presence that intrudes itself into [the] novel serves to belie the reportage that passes for historical records of this era" ("*Beloved*" 68). As a disembodied ghost at the outset of the novel, Beloved is the immaterial and elusive manifestation of the violence that slavery inspired. She is impossible to "line up" in any systematic taxonomy.

For contemporary readers, schoolteacher's efforts to maintain an objective and scientific method in classifying Sethe and its ultimate impact on the lives of all those he enslaves becomes the most uncanny, the most "gothic," dimensions of the text. Within the logic of Morrison's text, the system of slavery and the forms of brutality it produced under the rubric of Enlightenment thinking defies explanation in a way that Beloved's ghost does not. Even Sethe's murder of her child, itself a product of the slave system, receives extensive, albeit problematic explanation in the novel.

Schoolteacher's atrocities ultimately have no explanation. Far from opposed impulses, schoolteacher's enlightened rationality and the gothic novel in its traditional form work in tandem to obfuscate the ideological foundations of slavery.

Although at points I have argued that gothic elements in *Beloved* not only resist but defy interpretation, by retaining the spirit and the form of the gothic novel, Morrison retains the elements of horror that continue to resonate in our recent history. Ultimately, rather than reading the gothic as a system of symbols operating beneath the surface of the text, Morrison's complex orientation toward the form (much like Butler's orientation toward science fiction and Reed's stance on postmodern parody) encourages us to confront gothic elements as moments of intersection at the surface of the text. This does not mean, however, that postmodern slave narratives are flat texts without deep, symbolic resonance. In fact, these narratives call for a broader canvas of analysis that extends well beyond the texts themselves to include the cultural texts that produce particular discourses and modes of narrative representation. As a gothic novel, *Beloved*'s resistance to any one system of interpretation illustrates, more than anything else, that when African American writers of postmodern slave narratives confront an aesthetic form that has systematically silenced and obscured the history of slavery, that form must undergo a radical shift, a reflexive re-formation from the abstract realm of sliding signifiers and narrative play to the political realm of individual agency and historical authority.

Re-Forming Black Subjectivity

Symbolic Transculturation in Charles Johnson's *Oxherding Tale* and *Middle Passage*

S we have seen, the postmodern slave narratives by Reed, Butler, and
Morrison liberate the historical representation of slavery by dismantling traditional conceptions of history, realism, and objectivity. In
their place, these writers re-form the past by embracing literary forms and
genres traditionally associated with popular entertainment (the gothic),
escapism (speculative or science fiction), and political detachment (the
postmodern novel). Through the union of history, the fantastic, and oppositional politics, the contemporary author, the slave protagonist, and the
text itself claim an authority over the past that traditional history, realistic
historical novels, and postmodern texts cannot, or, in the case of the latter,
will not. Even a text like Ishmael Reed's *Flight to Canada,* marked as it is by
parodic, anachronistic, and at times ribald situations, assumes an authority over more traditional narratives through its critique of romanticized
depiction of the slave's search for freedom, its interrogation of black strategies for liberation, and its examination of slavery's legacy in postmodern
commodity culture. In contrast to the fractured, destabilized postmodern
subject, slave protagonists like Raven Quickskill, Dana Franklin, and even
Sethe, though battered and scarred by slavery, achieve an autonomy and
agency essential to a project of liberation. In turn, Reed, Butler, and
Morrison assert their authority to re-form the history of slavery through
their implied connection to the subject (both thematic and individual) of
their narratives. Far from deconstructing a unified concept of the black
subject and the black community, most writers of postmodern slave

narratives rely on a conception of a unified, coherent, and stable black identity in order to establish historical authority even as they undermine the mimetic conventions of traditional historical narratives. But what happens when the slave narrator as subject becomes the object of re-formation or postmodern deconstruction? What are the implications of using non-mimetic devices to depict an unstable and indeterminate black subject as opposed to an autonomous and stable one? The postmodern slave narratives by Charles Johnson force us to consider these questions and, as a result, shift the terms of critique established by the previous writers.

In *Oxherding Tale* (1982) and *Middle Passage* (1990), Charles Johnson struggles with an alternative vision of black subjectivity that undercuts the identity politics espoused by other writers I have examined thus far. Emphasizing the multiple and often conflicting cross-cultural influences instigated by slavery and the Atlantic slave trade, Johnson focuses on the transcultural aspect of black subjectivity and views identity not as a unitary or fixed entity but as "a process dominated by change and transformation" (Little, "Charles Johnson's Revolutionary *Oxherding Tale*," 165).[1] In an effort to avoid what he sees as the reductive trap of racial essentialism, Johnson re-forms the slave subject and, by extension, the nature of black subjectivity, by deconstructing the conventional first-person slave narrator so integral to the formal structure of the nineteenth-century slave narratives. Through a series of metafictional intrusions, philosophical digressions, and often parodic narrative situations, all of which undermine the autonomy and reliability of his protagonist, Johnson self-consciously draws attention to the first-person narrator; he critiques the device as both a convention of the slave narrative form and as a symbol of black subjectivity.[2] In re-forming the slave narrative, Johnson produces complex and hybrid texts that simultaneously use elements of the picaresque narrative, the comic novel, postmodern metafiction, and, of course, the slave narrative itself. In spite of this complexity, his novels push the boundaries of realism less overtly than other postmodern slave narratives I have examined. In place of material anachronism, time travel, and the gothic supernatural, Johnson emphasizes textuality and narrative form to undermine the realistic dimensions of his text. Even in the rare occasions when fantastic events occur (the seemingly omnipotent slave catcher Horace Bannon or the mythical African tribe the Allmuseri, for example) they are isolated moments in the text and are open to both literal and figurative interpretation. Nevertheless, these instances work in tandem with Johnson's preoccupation with literary form; the fantastic reinforces the disjuncture between Johnson's novels as textual constructs and the external history they depict. Johnson departs from the strategies other writers of the postmodern slave narrative employ. Whereas other postmodern slave narratives assert their narrative authority over the past, Johnson's narratives maintain a more postmodernist stance toward narrative historical representation by bracketing the text from the history it depicts.

Rather than using non-mimetic elements solely to liberate his slave protagonists (and contemporary readers) from the constraints of realism, Johnson uses these elements to liberate his protagonists from constraining definitions of black identity. His slave narrators, Andrew Hawkins (*Oxherding Tale*) and Rutherford Calhoun (*Middle Passage*), in both their actions as fictional characters and in their function as first-person narrators, reflect the complex, dispersed, and transcultural dimensions of their identities. Johnson's emphasis on transcultural subjectivity is a response to what he views as the black literary tradition's limited conceptions of black identity and its desire to place art in the service of ideology.[3] In *Being and Race,* Johnson criticizes the constraining ideological dimensions of the Harlem Renaissance and the Black Arts movement, two of the major African American literary and cultural movements of the twentieth century.[4] For Johnson, one significant limitation that arose out of these movements was the conception of an essentialist and authentic black identity. Such a conception, Johnson argues, marks a descent into ideology and can only result in intellectual, artistic, and philosophical stasis:

> The control and reconstitution, which arises out of the noble work of counteracting cultural lies, easily slips toward dogma that ends the process of literary discovery. . . . It cannot be through ideologies that genuine creative work is achieved. Rather, all presuppositions, all theories, must be suspended before experience and meaning can be brought forth in black literary art. (*Being* 29)

Johnson, more than any other writer I have discussed so far, rejects the elements of black cultural nationalism that, in some ways, inspired the reclamation of history in postmodern slave narratives. Even as he engages in a similar project as Reed, Butler, and Morrison, Johnson critiques their implicit claims of authority suggested by their texts. Although none of these writers explicitly identify with the Black Arts movement, all acknowledge the ideological foundations of their work and acknowledge their political identities as black writers. For Reed, Butler, and Morrison, the road to freedom for the contemporary author and the slave subject lies primarily in constructing a stable, politically autonomous communal sense of black identity in the face of the physical, psychological, and cultural sub-jugation of slavery and its legacy. For example, by the end of *Flight to Canada*, Uncle Robin resists the dehumanizing effects of white con-sumerism by hiring Raven to tell his story. For Dana Franklin, her trans-portation into the past forces her to acknowledge her history and cultural identity in ways she had previously ignored. In *Beloved*, Sethe's only hope for survival at the end of the novel is to relearn that she is "her own best thing."[5] In each of these instances, the key to liberation lies in the reclama-tion of a strong sense of black identity across time and space. By contrast, Johnson's goal as a writer is to preserve a distinction between the literary and the ideological and to free black creative expression from the limita-tions that ideology imposes. In advancing this goal, however, Johnson fails to acknowledge the ideology inherent in his own work; deconstructing racial essentialism in favor of a transcultural subjectivity constitutes an ideology in its own right—one that ultimately determines the ways Johnson rejects realism in order to expand the parameters of the slave nar-rative and black subjectivity. Where other authors turn to popular or con-temporary forms like science fiction, the gothic, or the postmodern novel, Johnson re-forms the slave narrative by explicitly examining the philo-sophical dimensions of the slave narrative itself. Johnson's preoccupation with the intertextual nature of narrative form in general, and his use of metafictional intrusion (*Oxherding Tale*) and allegory (*Middle Passage*) to examine it, emphasizes the fantastic dimensions intrinsic to the slave nar-rative as a form.

As a narrative construct and a representation of the individual slave subject, the slave narrator/protagonist operates at the site where literary form and ideological content explicitly converge in the slave narrative. In the original slave narrative and its contemporary counterpart, the slave narrator functions as a heroic cultural archetype—a politically driven fig-ure who achieves freedom in spite of all the obstacles in her way. In the act of narration, the former slave achieves both a sense of identity and an abil-ity to speak out against an institution that sought to suppress that identi-ty. Johnson undermines the heroic dimensions of Andrew Hawkins and Rutherford Calhoun as racial archetypes and focuses on their function as textual constructs.[6] This emphasis on the formal aspects of the slave nar-rative allows Johnson to relegate the sticky subject of ideology to the mar-gins of his novels. Nevertheless, Johnson's ideological project manifests itself in the very nature of his deconstruction of the slave narrator. For Johnson, identity itself is intertextual—the product of multiple and varied cultural traditions. As such, the historical impact of slavery and its legacy ultimately has more to do with the complex process of transculturation than with continued subjugation. Although Johnson does not deny the economic or physical abuses of slavery as a system, for him its legacy lies not in the lasting effects of these abuses but in the transculturation the Atlantic slave trade engendered. As a result, his texts (and his narrators) become playgrounds of transculturation and intertextuality that openly reveal and revel in a diverse range of sources and influences.

The foundation of Johnson's re-formation of the slave narrator lies in the textual representation and archetype of black subjectivity: the slave narrator. Johnson draws attention to the slave narrator's status as a textual construct most explicitly in one of the metafictional chapters of *Oxherding Tale*. In "The Manumission of First-Person Viewpoint," an authorial narrator, presumably Johnson, interrupts Andrew Hawkins's narrative in order to reflect on what he calls the slave narrative's "only invariant feature": the first-person viewpoint.[7] Johnson asserts, "what we value most highly in this viewpoint are precisely the limitations upon the narrator-perceiver. . . . [W]hat we lack in authority we gain in immediacy" (152). Johnson points out that an author, by granting readers access into a character's thoughts, produces the *illusion* of a speaking subject whose authority lies in his personal experience of slavery. Beyond the facade of a unified and autonomous individual who reports on the experience of slavery lies a formal convention of the text. Johnson states:

> The Self, this perceiving Subject who puffs on and on, is, for all purposes, a palimpsest, interwoven with everything—literally everything—that can be thought or felt. We can go further: The Subject of the Slave Narrative, like all Subjects, is forever *outside* itself in others, objects; he is parasitic, if you like, drawing his life from everything he is not, and at precisely the instant he makes possible their appearance. (152)

By drawing attention to the first-person narrator as a construction with a distinct form and function, Johnson strips the illusion of individual subjectivity and authority away. Johnson's metafictional intrusion, characteristic of many postmodern novels, emphasizes the purely textual and literary dimensions of the slave narrator and undermines a conception of the slave narrator as authentic (or, at the very least, authoritative) that other writers of postmodern slave narratives maintain. Johnson ends the chapter by stating, "having liberated the first-person, it is now only fitting that in the following chapters we do as much for Andrew Hawkins" (153). Liberating the first-person slave narrator from the constraints of narrative realism also allows him to liberate it from limiting conceptions of black identity and false claims of authority. For Johnson, both are forms of slavery.

Johnson's evocation of the palimpsest (a parchment or tablet that has been written upon or inscribed multiple times with the previous text or texts having been imperfectly erased and remaining still partly visible) as a metaphor for the slave narrator suggests that the perceiving subject of the slave narrative carries all the traces of those narrators and literary traditions that preceded it. The palimpsest operates as the symbol of the transcultural dimensions that each literary form and individual subject retains from its past. In *Being and Race,* Johnson returns to this image to illustrate the nature of language and the word, stating, "like a palimpsest, the word is a tissue of interpretation. Language is the experience, the sight . . . of others formed into the world" (39). In another metafictional chapter from *Oxherding Tale,* "On the Nature of Slave Narratives," Johnson argues that the slave narrative itself, grounded as it is in language, reflects the textual traces of its literary precursors much like a palimpsest. Rather than a product of a purely African American tradition, Johnson asserts:

> As a *form,* the . . . Slave Narrative is related, as distant cousins are related, to the Puritan Narrative. . . . In point of fact, the movement in the Slave Narrative from slavery (sin) to freedom (salvation) are identical to those of the Puritan Narrative, and *both* these genuinely American forms are the offspring of that hoary confession by the first philosophical black writer: Saint Augustine. . . . No form, I should note, loses its ancestry; rather, these meanings accumulate in layers of tissue as the form evolves. It is safe to conjecture that the Slave Narrative proper whistles and hums with this history. (118–19)

Emphasizing its intertextual and inherently transcultural characteristics, Johnson asserts that the slave narrative contains the forms and histories of those texts that preceded and influenced it. Johnson's inclusion of this metafictional chapter signals to the reader that his revision of the slave narrative explores not only the nature of black identity but also the historical and cultural dimensions of the form itself.

In his rejection of a racially essentialist view of the slave subject, Johnson presents us with an almost transcendental view of the slave narrator as textual construct. In this sense, Johnson departs from postmodern conceptions of narrative and subjectivity by positing an almost romantic or even Platonic view of narrative and literature. More than a representation of black subjectivity or even a narrative convention, Johnson views the first-person slave narrator as "an opening through which the world is delivered: first-person (if you wish) universal" (153).[8] However, it is important to acknowledge that, by drawing attention to and emphasizing the formal construction of the slave narrator, Johnson creates a tension between the text and an external reality that neither he nor we as readers can fully resolve. Although Andrew's and Rutherford's status as textual constructs allows him to expand our preconceived notions of the slave subject, as I will argue later in this chapter, Johnson cannot (and I suspect does not want to) escape the implications his revisions have on black identity external to the text.

As I have pointed out, in spite of his rejection of black nationalism and its ideological view of literature, Johnson's re-formation of the slave narrative constitutes its own ideology. In *Being and Race,* Johnson acknowledges the inevitability of ideology when he discusses the historical dimensions of literary form:

> No literary form is neutral. None is a value-empty vehicle into which we can simply "pour" the content of experience. . . . Each form, whether it be a fairy tale or a nonnarrative work, reveals a *Lebenswelt,* or vision of the world that is appropriate to its particular universe, and the use of any form will transfigure with startling results the "content" one wishes to express through it. (48)

Beyond an investigation into the slave narrative's textual history, Johnson's invocation of its form allows him to transfigure the content of the slave experience and to incorporate his own particular "vision of the world." Rather than an ideology of racial essentialism or an ideological conception of art, what emerges from Johnson's work, then, is an ideology of transculturation. Although his conception of the palimpsest as a metaphor for the transcultural dimensions of both black textuality and black identity seems idealistic, Johnson's preoccupation with slavery, as suggested by his two postmodern slave narratives, forces us to regard these concepts, in and of themselves, as multiple, complex, and historically determined. In spite of his emphasis on textuality and the nature of literary form, Johnson's re-formation of the slave narrative reveals the structures of power and domination inherent in the process of transculturation that is the byproduct of slavery. As a result, the metafictional and overtly allegorical dimensions of his texts (both non-mimetic in effect) allow Johnson to critique modes of narration that obscure the racial and historical complexities of black identity and black textuality.

Finding a Way: Transculturation in *Oxherding Tale*

One of the most disconcerting aspects of Johnson's postmodern slave narratives is their deconstruction of the boundary between the enslaver and the enslaved. Although Johnson's use of non-mimetic or fantastic elements never goes so far as to completely obscure or abstract the actual economy of the Atlantic slave trade, they do highlight the ways the processes of transculturation blur the lines between slave and master and between black and white identity. The crucial meeting that occurs early in *Oxherding Tale* between two prototypical characters of the slave narrative—the slave narrator and the slave catcher—illustrates this deconstruction. The interaction between the escaped slave, Andrew Hawkins, and Horace Bannon, the man hot on his trail, offers us two contrasting representations of transculturation and its impact on individual identity. By chance, Andrew Hawkins is introduced to Bannon, commonly referred to by those who fear him as the Soulcatcher. Infamous throughout the South, many believe that Bannon possesses the ability to consume the souls of the runaway slaves he has captured, a feat which allows him to intuit the actions and feelings of those slaves who try to elude him. This meeting foreshadows the critical role Bannon will play in Andrew's quest for freedom: the two will meet again in the final pages of the novel. But even in this initial meeting Johnson establishes Andrew and Bannon as parallel figures. Each must negotiate the violence of American slavery in order to achieve a sense of identity, however different their strategies as slave and slave catcher may be.

Upon his first meeting with Bannon, Andrew hides his identity by passing for white. As Andrew wears his ambiguous ancestry as a means of self-protection, he finds Bannon's racial ambiguity particularly striking:

> The Soulcatcher's voice, I swear, was black. The kind of deep-fried Mississippi Delta twang that magically turned floor into flow. Door into doe. [He was] a manhunter, a great, slack-shouldered monster with a gray Cathedral beard, a racial mongrel, like most Americans, but the genetic mix in the Soulcatcher was graphic: a collage of features that forced me, as he labored toward the door, looking down at me, the corners of his mouth turned up, to stare. Here the deltoid nose of a Wazimba, here "a snotcup" (so my stepmother called them) cut deeply above his lips, which were the sheerest line, slash; here curly hair coarsely textured like my father's; here heavy lidded eyes, one teal blue, one green beneath a low brow that bulged with veins. . . . I could not shake the feeling that Bannon was in masquerade, a slave who, for reasons too fantastic to guess, hunted slaves. (67–68)

By spending his life in pursuit of escaped slaves, Bannon has become a racial mongrel, appropriating the souls of those he has captured into his physical being. Whether we interpret the Soulcatcher's appearance in literal or symbolic terms, as a slave catcher of mixed ancestry (much as Andrew is a slave of mixed ancestry), or as a spiritual amalgamation of a multiracial and multicultural South, Bannon represents the violent intermixture of cultures and physical forms in graphic terms. Like Andrew, Bannon possesses the ability to masquerade as something he is not. However, because of Bannon's possible biraciality and Andrew's own racial intermixture, this "masquerade" might actually belie the palimpsestic aspects of American identity that arise out of slavery. Both men are transcultural in nature— graphically reflecting their entwined racial histories upon their facial features. Whereas Andrew stands at the crossroads of constructing a liberating transcultural identity in spite of his enslavement, Bannon has already developed a transcultural self, using it to enslave, consume, and destroy.

Johnson's use of these contrasting symbolic figures forces us to acknowledge that transculturation, in the context of American slavery, is always laden with some form of exertion, some form of power. Nowhere is this more evident than in the way Bannon uses his ability to incorporate black identity into his being as a means of capturing and killing escaped slaves. However, even as transculturation allows Bannon to consume and exploit more proficiently the minority cultures the slaves represent, this cross-cultural exchange also allows Andrew to manipulate a white Eurocentric culture that seeks to subjugate him. In each instance, transculturation involves an interplay of power relationships sometimes violently oppressive, sometimes empowering and liberating.

Although Johnson establishes Andrew and Bannon as parallel figures, Andrew's quest for a liberating identity in the face of American slavery is the primary subject of *Oxherding Tale*. At the outset of the novel, Andrew forces us to revise our expectations of his role as slave narrator and his representation of black identity. Drawing on one of the most basic and identifiable characteristics of the first-person slave narrative—the "I was born" statement that establishes the narrative as an autobiographical document—Andrew gives the reader an account of his origins. Although many of the original slave narrators are unable to identify one or both of their parents, Andrew, recalling Sterne's comic narrator *Tristram Shandy,* identifies the moment of his conception.[9] Andrew narrates this moment in ribald fashion, speculating on the drunken exchange of wives between his father, George Hawkins, a field slave, and Jonathan Polkinghorne, the slave owner. In contrast to the suggestions of violence and sexual abuse that run as an undercurrent through many slave narratives, Andrew refers to his origins with humor and irony, characterizing George and Jonathan's exchange as a comedy of errors. Johnson transforms the voice of the slave narrator from one of impassioned protest against the depravities of slavery to one of humorous speculation. Unlike Reed who overtly undermines the realistic dimensions of his text through the parodic use of material anachronism, Johnson forces us to straddle the line between realism and the fantastic. Although certainly possible, Andrew's conception and his characterization of it represent such a marked departure from other narrative accounts of slavery that it reinforces the novel's status as a textual construct.

Even more than the system of slavery itself, the central dilemma for Andrew is his quest to achieve a liberating subjectivity unconstrained by racial ideology. As a product of the union between George Hawkins and Polkinghorne's wife, Anna, Andrew views himself as marginalized—an individual belonging "to both house and field . . . but popular in neither" (8). Light-complexioned with Caucasian features, Andrew, like Horace Bannon, bears the traces of a transcultural identity in his physical being. In spite of his ability to pass as white, Andrew's status as a slave prevents him from achieving a liberated sense of identity that is based on his physical appearance.[10] Confused by his inability to fully embrace either cultural heritage, Andrew spends the length of the novel searching for a way to integrate these conflicting forces into a transcultural identity. One of Andrew's first obstacles is the complicated question of paternity. Because Andrew identifies with both Polkinghorne and George as father figures, the reality of his mixed ancestry fragments his identity rather than liberates it. George Hawkins enhances Andrew's confusion by not only voicing a contempt for the white culture that has enslaved him but also by essentializing Andrew's identity in what Andrew himself sees as a limiting conception of race:

> More than anything else, I wanted my father's approval—I did, in fact, clomp along in his boots when I was a child, but he was so bitter. And his obsession with the world-historical mission of Africa? I didn't want this obligation! How strange that my father, the skillful, shrewd, funny, and wisest butler at Cripplegate . . . was beneath his mask of good humor and harmlessness a flinty old Race Man. (21)

George espouses a racially essentialist and politically militant view of identity (one that recalls the black cultural nationalism that Johnson critiques in *Being and Race*) that Andrew finds constraining. Ultimately he rejects

George's worldview and sets out to construct an identity that reflects his mixed racial ancestry and a broader range of cultural influence. In essence, Andrew views his own identity as a palimpsest.

Andrew experiences an even greater conflict as a result of his formal education. Under the tutelage of Ezekiel Sykes-Withers, a transcendentalist scholar Jonathan Polkinghorne hires to educate him, Andrew follows "a program modeled on that of James Mill for his son John Stuart" (12). Inspired by the Scottish philosopher's classical and rigorous model, Sykes-Withers teaches Andrew texts in both the Eastern and Western philosophical traditions, encouraging him to learn Greek and to read works by Xenophon and Plato, Lao Tzu, and Chuang Tzu. At first, Andrew attacks his studies voraciously, rapidly consuming these Eastern and Western canonical texts. Eventually, however, Andrew begins to notice the discrepancies between the abstract ideas of these philosophies and his circumstances as a slave: "Soon all life left my studies . . . these vain studies of things moral, things transcendental, things metaphysical were, all in all, rich food for the soul, but in Cripplegate's quarters all that was considered as making life worth living was utterly wanting" (13). Although Andrew embraces some aspects of transcultural identity (as exemplified by his passion for these philosophical texts), his status as a slave renders most of them inconsequential. In fact, the process of transculturation, at this stage in his life, renders him nearly incapable of integrating the diverse aspects of his life into a sense of identity.

An example of Andrew's struggles as a result of his classical education occurs in one of his philosophical diversions in the text. Contemplating the long standing racial conflict between George Hawkins and Jonathan Polkinghorne, Andrew reflects on these tensions by posing philosophical questions on the nature of Man and his relationship to the heart. As he traces the etymology of the word from its Sanskrit origin to its current usage, he ultimately concludes that the heart's meaning lies "at precisely the point where Matter and Mind, spirit and flesh, heaven and earth, subject and object, Self and Other, locked like fingers" (28). Realizing that his abstract reflections and his education in Eastern and Western philosophy has led him astray in sufficiently explaining the complexities of slavery and racial politics, Andrew admits: "Perhaps the narratives of Gustavus Vassa and Venture Smith are, as confessions, clearer about slavery and sexual politics, but I (alas) was lost in the ideas at Cripplegate" (28–29). Andrew realizes that the process of achieving a liberated identity lies beyond the consumption of cultural texts and an immersion in the rigors of a classical education. Following the example of Sykes-Withers forces Andrew to examine the implication of a transcultural intellectualism that fails to address or incorporate the realities of his position as a slave. Ironically, the abstract transcendentalism that characterizes Ezekiel Sykes-Withers recalls Johnson's own view of the transcendent dimensions of language and fiction. Both stances obfuscate the ideological forces at work in Andrew's status as a slave and as a slave narrator.

Shortly after reaching this impasse in his search for a liberating identity, Andrew asks Polkinghorne for his freedom. Instead, Polkinghorne sends him to Leviathan, the plantation owned by Flo Hatfield. At Leviathan and under the tutelage of Flo Hatfield, Andrew experiences another limited (and limiting) model of transcultural identity. Flo, a woman of voracious sexual appetites, chooses Andrew as her sex slave and instructs him in the erotic arts. Even as her sexual prowess seduces him, Andrew realizes that Flo limits his identity as she consumes his body for pleasure; just as Bannon consumes slaves by hunting them down and killing them, Flo Hatfield uses sex as a means of incorporating her slaves into her self-conception. When Andrew learns that he is one of many slaves Flo has consumed (and eventually discarded), he realizes that, in its many guises, the harsh reality of slavery continuously reduces his identity to the surface of his skin:

> Although anything you said about slavery could be denied in the same breath, this much struck me as true: the wretchedness of being colonized was not that slavery created feelings of guilt and indebtedness, though I did feel guilt and debt, nor that it created a long lurid dream of multiplicity and separateness, which it indeed created, but the fact that men had epidermalized Being. The Negro—one Negro at Leviathan—was needed as meaning. So it was; so it was. (52)

Although he suffered constraints upon his identity at Cripplegate because of his marginal status (between both house and field) and his ineffectual education, Flo's conception of race undermines his goal of a liberated and transcultural self to an even greater extent. Much as George's stance of racial essentialism defines black identity in vague and one-dimensional terms, Flo's view of race restricts Andrew to one role. Once again Andrew must seek out an alternative, multidimensional conception of identity.

In order to escape slavery and Flo's personal hold over him, Andrew flees Leviathan with Reb, a fellow slave on the plantation. As a member of the Allmuseri, a fictional African tribe that Johnson develops in his later novel *Middle Passage*, Reb represents an Africanist worldview that stresses the intersubjective links between members of the community. Part of this

view of identity suggests a relinquishing of any individual desires that separate one from the group.[11] As he reflects on Reb's conception of selfhood,
it is clear that, although he admires him, Andrew cannot accept his view as
his own:

> Reward [Reb] did not expect. Nor pleasure. Desire was painful. Duty was
> everything—the casket promised tomorrow, a carving for the blacksmith's
> daughter, the floorboards that needed fixing. This was his Way. It was, I
> thought, a Way of strength and spiritual heroism . . . but like Flo Hatfield's
> path of the senses, it was not my Way. (77)

Andrew, in spite of his existence on the margins between house and field,
between the white world and the black world, does not want to remain
separate from either identity. Rather, Andrew's quest is for a liberated sense
of self in the face of slavery and the complex forces of transculturation.

Only toward the end of the novel, after he passes for white, assumes the
name William Harris, and marries Peggy Underhill, a white woman, does
Andrew realize which ontology most suits his identity. He states:

> I had seen so many Ways since leaving Hodges—the student in Ezekiel, the
> senses in Flo Hatfield, the holy murderer in Bannon (Shiva's hitman), and
> Reb, who was surely a Never-Returner; but in all these well-worn trails—
> none better than another—I discovered that my dharma, such as it was,
> was that of a householder. (147)

Rather than a state of detachment, strength, or spiritual heroism, what
Andrew desires more than anything else is a state of domestic bliss.
Interestingly, Andrew fashions his "Way" based on the model of Karl Marx
who appears as a character earlier in the text. Based on his experiences with
him on the plantation at Cripplegate, he views Marx in a way that is quite
different from our view of the historical materialist. Describing Marx he
writes: "Marx . . . did not live for ideas, political or otherwise; he was, in the
old sense—the Sanskrit sense—a householder. [T]he humorless student
radical of the 1830s was—you cannot guess—a citizen devoted, first and
foremost, to his family" (84).[12] In essence, Andrew has become a Marxist as
defined by the fictional context of the novel. It is through Marx's sense of
self, a phenomenological one that requires the domestic merger with an
essential other—that Andrew has found a Way. However, Andrew's construction of a liberated, transcultural self is flawed. In order to achieve his
role as a householder he must break an earlier promise to George that he

would never relinquish his identity as a black man. Although Andrew achieves his freedom through these means, his model of transculturation descends into a politically and culturally limited form of assimilation. The price for freedom and domestic bliss is his black identity.

Ironically, the person who understands Andrew's conception of self most is Horace Bannon, the Soulcatcher. When he encounters Bannon for the final time in the novel, Andrew is still a fugitive slave passing for white. Giving every indication that he recognizes him from Flo Hatfield's plantation, Bannon explains to Andrew his process of capturing escaped slaves, stating: "You become a Negro by lettin' yoself see what he sees, feel what he feels, want what he wants" (115). Bannon points out that what escaped slaves want is respectability, "to be able to walk down the street and be unnoticed" (115). The desire for ordinariness (or, in Andrew's case, assimilation) allows Bannon to capture those slaves who try their best to look average, which ultimately makes Andrew vulnerable to him. The primary obstacle in Andrew's domestic bliss, then, is the Soulcatcher—his counterpart as a symbol of transculturation.

In the final chapter of the novel, entitled "Moksha" (meaning "enlightenment" or "liberation"), Andrew and the Soulcatcher stand together in a moment that recalls their first meeting. In their final confrontation, Bannon tells Andrew that he has decided to retire from his life as a slave catcher. In his retirement, Bannon, like Andrew, has settled into a life of domestic bliss with his new wife, a former prostitute named Minnie. In a final gesture of truce, Bannon allows Andrew to speak to his father whom Bannon had captured and killed. It is in this moment that Johnson's text stretches the boundaries of realism most explicitly. Unbuttoning and opening his shirt, Bannon reveals to Andrew the graphic representation of his transcultural essence:

> [His chest was] an impossible tapestry of a thousand individuals no longer static, mere drawings, but if you looked at them long enough, bodies moving like Lilliputians across the surface of his skin. Not tattoos at all, I saw, but forms sardined in his contour, creatures Bannon had killed since childhood . . . even the tiniest of these thrashings within the body mosaic was clearly a society as complex as the higher forms, a concrescence of molecules cells atoms in concert, for nothing in the necropolis stood alone, wished to stand alone, had to stand alone, and the commonwealth of the dead shape-shifted on his chest . . . their metamorphosis having no purpose beyond the delight the universe took in diversity for its own sake. (175)

Bannon's body represents a violent democracy of souls in which diversity, brought together by a consumptive force of slavery, struggles to cohere in one transcultural form. As James Coleman points out, the tapestry of souls reveals that Bannon "is this amoral inexorable process that is past, present, and future, and thus he symbolizes part of Johnson's intertextual process" (636). Like Johnson's re-formation of the slave narrative itself, Bannon's body is a palimpsest of American slavery. Its surface contains the multitudinous voices of those consumed by slavery. Just as Andrew finds his identity by successfully negotiating transculturation, Bannon, too, is free to lead a new life carrying its graphic manifestation, albeit in a darker and more disturbing form.

What does Johnson have in mind when he posits these two characters together within this framework of liberation and enlightenment? Perhaps even more important, what does it mean that Bannon can achieve a sense of liberation after he has destroyed the lives of so many? This symbolic image allows Johnson to acknowledge the realistic aspects of transculturation, the tandem of violence and liberation inherent in its inner workings. The fact that both Andrew and Bannon construct their lives anew by the end of the novel, both marrying and leading domestic lives, suggests that both of these forces are ever at work not only within the historical moment of slavery but in its legacy. By having both Andrew and Bannon achieve a sense of liberation, we are forced to view transculturation through a dual lens, one that renders the phenomenon as both liberating and constraining in its diversity.

Charles Johnson's examination of transculturation and Andrew's quest for a liberating identity, however, remain not only unresolved but also mired in Eurocentric racial ideology. Although Andrew successfully escapes re-enslavement and is free to continue his life with his wife, Peggy Underhill, in order to do this he must continue to pass as white. He must relinquish a fundamental component of his transcultural identity. Although such a solution works for Andrew as a textual construct, the implications of this are problematic at best. Even as Johnson succeeds in liberating the form and function of the slave narrator, he raises even more complex questions regarding the nature of black identity in the wake of slavery and the dynamics of transculturation it produces in American culture. *Oxherding Tale,* in spite of itself, ends pessimistically. Rather than positing a subjectivity unconstrained by racial categories, Johnson's textual solution falls back into a black-white binary that serves as one of the conceptual foundations of American slavery.

The Slave Narrative As Allegory:
Transculturation in *Middle Passage*

Johnson's second re-formation of the slave narrative, *Middle Passage*, addresses the same complexities of transculturation (both cultural and textual) and reveals the same limitations as *Oxherding Tale*. In many ways, *Middle Passage* is an extension of the previous novel, reflecting Johnson's interest in intertextuality and its impact on both individual and cultural identity. Although *Middle Passage* contains no overt metafictional intrusions, the numerous intertextual references, both implicit and explicit, allow Johnson to re-form the slave narrative as an allegory—one that brackets the text from narrative realism as much as other postmodern slave narratives.

Rather than symbolizing the processes of transculturation through individual characters in the novel, Johnson places two communities in opposition to each another. The *Republic,* an American slave ship, and the Allmuseri tribe, a group of Africans brought on board, represent opposing cultural archetypes of the Middle Passage, just as Andrew Hawkins and Horace Bannon represent the archetypes of the slave narrative. The *Republic* stands for the colonizing aspects of Western culture as a whole whereas the Allmuseri represent an idealized version of African culture, untainted by the influences of the West. By treating the slave vessel and the Allmuseri tribe as symbols, Johnson places two worldviews in opposition and examines the impact each has on the other. However, Johnson still concerns himself primarily with the nature of identity by filtering his narrative through the first-person perspective of a (former) slave narrator. Although a free man at the time of his experiences on the *Republic,* Rutherford Calhoun still represents the archetypal slave narrator who searches for his identity amidst a culture that defines and limits him. As a free black man, Rutherford is neither a member of the community of enslavers on board the *Republic* nor a part of the African tribal community they enslave. Much like Andrew Hawkins existed between house and field, Rutherford stands between Africa and America, ultimately witnessing the violent conflict between them from a marginal position. As both a character and a symbol in the text, Rutherford, by the end of the novel, represents the problematic and potentially liberating results of transculturation even out of its violent shards. Through him Johnson reconceptualizes the concept of a transcultural identity, wrought by the conflict of slavery and the Atlantic slave trade.

The *Republic's* status as both a cultural symbol and a textual element is evident immediately through its reference to the philosophical text by Plato. In *The Republic,* Socrates asserts that justice cannot be found in the individual until it has been found in the State. He conceptualizes a State in which citizens are divided into three classes: the guardians, the soldiers, and the workers. In order for political justice and stability to exist, each group must be confined to its proper social function. By invoking this intertextual reference, Johnson places his text and the *Republic* squarely in the Western tradition, encouraging us to interpret his novel as a treatise on the individual, the state, and social justice. As a slave vessel, the *Republic* functions as a makeshift State. With a captain (Ebenezer Falcon), a first mate (Peter Cringle), a crew, and a cargo of slaves as commodities, the *Republic* clearly operates under a hierarchical system. However, as the events of the novel progress, it becomes clear that the structural system under which the *Republic* functions is anything but stable or just.

In the beginning of the novel, Rutherford stows away on board the vessel in order to escape an arranged marriage to Isadora Bailey, a woman who wants to "civilize" him. A thief, a wanderer, and a liar, Rutherford resembles a picaro as much as a traditional slave narrator, using his wits for survival like a trickster figure. Upon seeing the *Republic* for the first time, however, Rutherford is disturbed by its image:

> I had an odd sensation, difficult to explain, that I'd boarded not a ship but a kind of fantastic, floating Black Maria, a wooden sepulcher whose timbers moaned with the memory of too many runs of black gold between the New World and the Old; moaned, I say again, because the ship—with its tiered compartments and galleys, like a crazy quilt-house built by a hundred carpenters, each with a different plan—felt conscious and disapprovingly aware of my presence. (21)

The physical product of a collective of carpenters and containing the memory of countless voyages along the Atlantic slave trade, the *Republic* seems to embody slavery itself. From the moment he finds himself on board, Rutherford realizes that his wits have brought him to the wrong place.

Once on board, the ship's first mate, Peter Cringle, discovers Rutherford and puts him to work as the cook's helper. Although all, from Captain Falcon to the crew, accept Rutherford's presence, they never fully incorporate him into the community of the ship. From Rutherford's vantage point, the *Republic* appears as an amalgam of disparate parts, containing men from different regions of the world and different social classes. Far from a perfectly coherent or stable community, the *Republic*, as both a ship and as a representation of Western culture, threatens to literally and figuratively come apart:

> The *Republic* was physically unstable. She was perpetually flying apart and re-forming during the voyage, falling to pieces beneath us. . . . Captain Falcon's crew spent most of their time literally rebuilding the *Republic* as we crawled along the waves. In a word, she was, from stem to stern, a process. (35–36)

In spite of its instability, the crew is able to work together to keep the vessel from breaking apart. For the time, the ship and the crew are able to construct a community out of its disunity of parts.

As the captain of the vessel, Ebenezer Falcon rules much like a despot, representing and instilling a tenuous order for the ship and crew. Falcon's worldview dominates the *Republic* and moves it toward the African shore where they will "obtain" slaves and African artifacts for the New World. Rutherford describes Falcon as a strong and able man despite his short, almost dwarflike stature. For Rutherford, he embodies "that special breed of empire builder, explorer, and imperialist that sculptors like to elongate . . . whose burning passion was the manifest destiny of the United States to Americanize the planet" (29–30). Falcon represents the cultural and textual symbol of the slave merchant. His presence in the text serves as the voice of the slave system as a whole. Guided by profit, Falcon ultimately seeks not only to enslave the Allmuseri tribe but also to pilfer its culture, even going so far as to steal their god. Like Bannon in *Oxherding Tale* and even Yankee Jack in *Flight to Canada,* Falcon consumes black culture as a way of Being.

When both the Allmuseri slaves who plot revolt and the mutinous faction of the crew who reject his authority challenge Falcon's control over the *Republic* on each side, Rutherford is struck by the calmness of his demeanor. For Falcon, conflict defines being:

> For a self to act, it must have somethin' to act *on*. A nonself—some call this Nature—that resists thwarts the will, and *vetoes* the actor. May I proceed? Well suppose that nonself is another self? What then? As long as each sees a situation differently there will be slaughter and slavery and the subordination of one to another 'cause two notions of things never exist side by side as equals. . . . The reason—the irrefragable truth is each person in his heart believes *his* beliefs is best. Fact is, down deep no man's democratic.

> We're closet anarchists, I'd wager. . . . Conflict . . . is what it means to be
> conscious. Dualism is a bloody structure of the mind. Subject and object,
> perceiver and perceived, self and other—these ancient twins are built into
> the mind like the stem-piece of a merchantman. (97–98)

Falcon reiterates the natural "truth" of the Cartesian split between mind
and matter that forms the basis of Western reason. The result of this split,
he insists, is the perpetual struggle between people and cultures.
Rutherford, broken down by his own failure to resist either Falcon's
authority or the pull of the mutineers, can think of no response to counter
Falcon's view. He is trapped between conflicting worldviews and is unable
to define himself apart from or even within them.

In many ways the Allmuseri represent both the antithesis of Falcon's
dualist philosophy and the cultural embodiment of Johnson's concept of
transcultural identity. As Ashraf Rushdy points out, the Allmuseri provide,
for all the American characters in Johnson's novels, "an ideal of intersubjective relations" that pose a solution to the dilemma of being caught
between Africa and Europe (376). In other words, for Rutherford specifically, the Allmuseri represent a particular way of Being that will allow him
to locate his identity. Upon his first encounter with the tribe, Rutherford
sees them as an ancient people who reach back to the origins of humanity:

> You felt they had run the full gamut of civilized choices, or played through
> every political or social possibility and now had nowhere to go. . . .
> Physically, they seemed a synthesis of several tribes, as if longevity in this
> land had made them a biological repository of Egyptian and sub-Saharan
> eccentricities or—in the Hegelian equation—a clan distilled from every-
> thing that came earlier. Put another way, they might have been the Ur-tribe
> of humanity itself. (61)

The Allmuseri are the physical and cultural embodiment of the
palimpsest—a text of humanity that contains the traces of all the cultures
with which they have come into contact. In essence, as a people, they
accomplish in their physical being that which Falcon and the *Republic* try
to achieve by raiding Africa of its cultural artifacts.

A part of Rutherford wishes he could join the tribe and take part in
their cultural traditions. He realizes, however, almost as much as the white
crew of the *Republic,* that the distance between his cultural identity and
theirs is vast. In fact, to the Allmuseri, the Europeans on the *Republic* (and
even to a certain extent Rutherford himself) are barbarians:

> They saw us as savages. In their mythology Europeans had once been members of their tribe—rulers, even, for a time—but fell into what was for these people the blackest of sins. The failure to experience the unity of Being everywhere was the Allmuseri vision of Hell. And that was where we lived: purgatory. That was where we were taking them—into the madness of multiplicity—and the thought of it drove them wild. (65)

The "madness of multiplicity" is the result of Falcon's (and Western culture's) dualistic worldview—an ontology based on the separation between self and other. Even in terms of their spoken language, the Allmuseri reject the dualistic split between subject and object, between signifier and signified, by reducing the number of nouns in their lexicon. Of their written language, which consists of pictograms that could be grasped "in a single intuitive snap," Rutherford states, "It was not, I gathered a good language for doing analytic work, or deconstructing things into discrete parts" (77–78).

Johnson posits the Allmuseri as the ancient Ideal in the novel, and like most Ideals, they falter when confronted by the conflicted world of the Real. The dehumanizing atrocities of the Middle Passage, of being stripped of their homes and community, inevitably takes its toll on the Allmuseri who survive most of the voyage. In fact, because the Allmuseri's ontology is one that incorporates the cultural identities of those they encounter, it renders them even more susceptible to the conflicts inherent in the worldview that Falcon and the *Republic* represent. Witnessing the ways the Middle Passage subtly changed Ngonyama, one of the Allmuseri, Rutherford realizes that their culture was, much like the *Republic,* a process:

> Stupidly, I had seen their lives and culture as timeless product, a finished thing, pure essence or Parmenidean meaning I envied and wanted to embrace, when the truth was that they were process and Heraclitean change, like any men, not fixed but evolving. . . . Ngonyama and, maybe all the Africans, I realized, were not wholly Allmuseri anymore. We changed them. I suspected even he did not recognize the quiet revisions in his voice after he learned English as it was spoken by the crew, or how the vision hidden in their speech was deflecting or redirecting his own way of seeing. (124)

Johnson suggests that even in the subtle changes of words and speech, the process of transculturation works upon the Allmuseri. In this instance, transculturation is the product of the violent and exploitative forces of slavery. It is the manifestation of power being exerted by one culture over another. Even when the Allmuseri successfully rise up and revolt against Captain Falcon and his crew, they cannot reverse the effects of transculturation. In fact, as Rutherford notes, even in the very act of resistance and victory, the Allmuseri have taken in Falcon's worldview, becoming part of the conflict that comes out of multiplicity (140).

Rutherford, more a witness than an active participant in the Allmuseri revolt on the *Republic,* documents the events in the ship's log. And yet, even he cannot avoid the effects of transculturation that come as a result of his interactions with both the American crew of the *Republic* and the African tribe. In fact, his state of liminality, caught between two cultures neither of which he is a part, allows each world to act upon him with equal force. Whereas Rutherford had experienced a sense of marginality and displacement before his life on the *Republic,* he begins to accept a more liberating sense of transculturation as he learned it from the Allmuseri. As the survivors of the revolt drift at sea, Rutherford reflects on his state of being:

> I peered deep into memory and called forth all that had ever given me solace, scraps and rags of language too, for in myself I found nothing I could rightly call Rutherford Calhoun, only pieces and fragments of all the people who had touched me, all the places I had seen, all the homes I had broken into. The 'I' that I was, was a mosaic of many countries, a patchwork of others and objects stretching backward to perhaps the beginning of time. (162–63)

Although this loss of self in the mosaic of other cultures comes at a time when Rutherford clings to life, it represents a pathway to a liberated and transcultural identity.

Perhaps the moment that most represents Rutherford's liberated sense of self comes when he is chosen to feed the Allmuseri god Captain Falcon has stolen and keeps in a cage on the lower decks. Like an ancient oracle, the god reveals itself to Rutherford in the form of his deceased father who had abandoned him as a boy. The Allmuseri god, like Soulcatcher, contains the voices of the multitude of people and cultures it has experienced. Rutherford's father appears as both one and many:

> But even in death [my father] seemed to be doing something, or perhaps should I say he squeezed out one final cry wherethrough I heard a cross wind of sounds just below his breathing. A thousand soft undervoices that

jumped my jangling sense from his last, weakly syllabled wind to a mosaic of voices within voices, each one immanent in the other, none his but all strangely his, the result being that as the loathsome creature, this deity from the dim beginnings of the black past, folded my father back into the broader, shifting field—as waves vanish into water—his breathing blurred in a dissolution of sounds and I could only feel that identity was imagined; I had to listen harder to isolate him from the We that swelled each particle and pore of him, as if the (black) self was the greatest of all fictions; and then I could not find him at all. He seemed everywhere, his presence, and that of countless others, in me as well as the chamber which had suddenly changed. Suddenly I knew the god's name: Rutherford. (170)

A true symbol of transculturation and intersubjectivity, the Allmuseri god reflects multiplicity in harmony in a way that the *Republic* could never create. Rutherford, as a result of hearing the multitude, views his sense of self differently, learning to accept the many cultures that make up his identity: "The voyage had irreversibly changed my seeing, made of me a cultural mongrel, and transformed the world into a fleeting shadow play I felt no need to posses or dominate, only appreciate in the ever extended present" (187).

Johnson ends *Middle Passage* in a similar fashion as *Oxherding Tale:* in domestic bliss. One of only a handful of survivors of the *Republic,* Rutherford is rescued by an American ship. With his new sense of a liberated and transcultural identity, he eventually marries Isadora Bailey and adopts an orphaned Allmuseri child named Baleka. In essence, Rutherford has achieved the "householder" identity much like his counterpart, Andrew Hawkins. For both characters, the difficult process of finding a liberated transcultural self amidst the violent and power-laden forces of transculturation results in a sense of integration on both a personal and a cultural level.

Charles Johnson's re-formation of the slave narrative and his interrogation into the nature of transculturation allow him to construct a seemingly optimistic conception of a post-slavery identity for his protagonists. But he leaves us with an incomplete picture. Rutherford has survived the Middle Passage and relinquished a life of petty crimes, but he also suffers the loss of the Allmuseri tribe who perished with the destruction of the *Republic.* As a result, he is unable to sexually consummate his union with Isadora. Johnson ends the novel with Rutherford and Isadora proclaiming a sexless and platonic love for one another. In *Oxherding Tale,* Andrew has successfully escaped re-enslavement by the Soulcatcher and is free to continue his life with his wife, Peggy Underhill. However, in order to do this, Andrew must continue to pass as white, thus relinquishing a fundamental component of his transcultural identity. The fact that Johnson leaves his characters content but not fully resolved suggests that transculturation and the struggles for a post-slavery identity is still a work-in-process. In many ways, other postmodern slave narratives end with a similar ambivalence. In both *Kindred* and *Beloved,* the protagonists still suffer the residual effects of slavery that complicate their lives. We are uncertain if Dana Franklin's marriage will survive its confrontation with the past. We can only hope that Sethe will stop contemplating colors and resist a fate like Baby Suggs by leaving her sick bed. In fact, many of the original slave narratives also leave us with a similar open-endedness regarding the prospects of a post-slavery identity in a country that still supports such a system. However, Andrew and Rutherford's contentment at the end of their narratives suggests an acceptance of their limited identities. This seems at odds with Johnson's ideological project. The possibility of a post-slavery identity that goes beyond the racial divide of black and white lies, as we will see, in an even greater re-formation of the slave narrative and a more radical rejection of realism.

Beyond Postmodernity

De-familiarizing the Postmodern Slave Narrative

A s we have seen, the rejection of realism as the primary mode of historical narrative simultaneously proclaims the writer's ability to reexamine the slave experience and to achieve narrative authority without the constraints of verisimilitude. The authority, then, lies not in an ability to authenticate or replicate the past, but in the act of eroding traditional narrative conventions. Contemporary writers set out to defamiliarize the slave narrative. However, even as they reject realism as a narrative mode, all the novels I have discussed so far still retain some basic elements of realism. In fact, the real and the fantastic exist in conjunction with each other, setting each other in bold relief. In this chapter, I want to examine two texts that stretch the boundaries of realism and the conventions of the slave narrative even farther, to the point, even, where such boundaries explode. Jewelle Gomez's collection of vampire tales *The Gilda Stories* (1991) and Samuel R. Delany's science fiction novel *Stars in My Pocket like Grains of Sand* (1984) represent the most radical re-formations of the slave narrative. Much as Morrison re-formed the gothic novel by grounding it in the history of slavery, Gomez and Delany "historicize" two popular genres that many have regarded, until recently, as escapist and a-historical. By using these genres to project the legacy of slavery into the future, Gomez and Delany defamiliarize not only the original slave narrative form but also its contemporary counterpart.

The fact that Gomez and Delany combine the slave narrative with such popular and familiar narrative forms as the vampire tale (*The Gilda*

Stories) and the science fiction novel (*Stars*) complicates the process of defamiliarizing readers. On one hand, the slave narrative in its original form relies on a certain degree of realism to depict history. On the other hand, the vampire tale (with its depiction of the "undead" and the violent, yet sensual act of feeding on human blood) and science fiction (with its tropes of time and space travel, futuristic technologies, and alien species) typically rely on the fantastic to displace history. In addition, although the tropes of science fiction and the vampire tale are fantastic in nature, the genres themselves are highly conventionalized depictions of alternative realities. As a result, novels in these genres tend to displace questions of realism and verisimilitude without narrative tension. The process of defamiliarizing readers in *Stars* and *The Gilda Stories*, then, involves not simply the use of science fiction and the vampire tale; it requires a fusion of these genres with the history of slavery and the slave narrative. The mixture of genres—each recognizable and conventional on its own—results in complex, hybrid texts. In essence, *The Gilda Stories* and *Stars* rely on conjunction of the familiar, the conventional, the historical, and the contemporary in order to defamiliarize the narrative representation of slavery.

Part of the defamiliarization at work in these texts comes from the somewhat marginalized status of Delany and Gomez as writers. In many ways, both authors write between audiences. As African American writers of fantastic popular fiction, Gomez and Delany work within genres that, until recently, have been largely the province of white, heterosexual males.[1] Lando Calrissian and Blacula aside, most science fiction and vampire narratives continue to reflect a homogeneous audience in their dearth of black characters and their limited discussions of race.[2] Significantly, both Gomez and Delany choose to use slavery as the means to project blackness into the future. Their "future" is one grounded in a particular history. As black writers who have written in these popular genres, Gomez and Delany have also been undervalued by critics within the African American literary tradition.[3] Their marginalization intersects in interesting ways with the emergence of postmodernism and the "canon wars" of the 1970s and 80s. With the rise of postmodernism and cultural studies, the academy embraced popular genres like science fiction as objects of critical analysis, thus blurring the lines between the popular and the literary. As the canon opened up to popular genres, black critics and other writers of color also fought for and found greater representation in the canon. However, this contested process coincided with the rising prominence of African American academics who embraced post-structuralist literary theory and focused their analyses on writers of "high art." As a result, African American texts "admitted" into the canon during this time were primarily literary rather than popular.[4] This phenomenon, coupled with the fact that science fiction and the vampire tale had historically marginalized both black readers and black writers, contributed to their limited popularity and critical acceptance. Although this has started to change, in the early 1980s to the early 1990s (when these particular texts were originally published), Gomez and Delany were writing in forms that excluded them from most discussions of African American literature in ways that did not affect more prominent and accepted writers of postmodern slave narratives like Morrison, Reed, and Johnson.

Perhaps as a result of this double marginalization, both *The Gilda Stories* and *Stars* advance a conception of black identity that stands apart not only from traditional science fiction and vampire narratives but also from other postmodern slave narratives. Where other postmodern slave narratives resist, to varying degrees, an essentialist conception of black identity, Gomez and Delany outwardly undermine this conception by promoting an expansive radical black subjectivity only hinted at in Charles Johnson's texts. Gomez and Delany create characters whose complex identities reflect the possibilities and challenges beyond a postmodern world. Where texts like *Kindred* and *Flight to Canada* use non-mimetic elements to project the legacy of slavery into the present, the expansiveness of science fiction and the vampire tale allow *The Gilda Stories* and *Stars* to project the legacy of slavery into the future. In *The Gilda Stories*, Gomez's protagonist escapes slavery with the help of a woman who turns her into a vampire. Once transformed, Gilda carries her experiences with slavery into the mid-twenty-first century. In the case of Delany's novel, echoes of American slavery resonate into a futuristic and intergalactic landscape— one distant in time and space from our own. From this vantage point, Delany contextualizes his narrative within the history of slavery primarily through his protagonist, Rat Korga, who escapes slavery and annihilation on a distant and alien world. As a result of the expanded narrative landscapes of these genres, the slave and postslave experience these texts depict have less to do with the impact of slavery on black/white relations and more to do with the increased complexity of global and multicultural politics, expanded definitions of sexual identity, and vast advancements in science and technology. These texts create radical definitions of difference, otherness, and humanity in a way that other postmodern slave narratives, grounded in the slave experience as they are, cannot. What emerges, then, is a conception of identity and community that relies not on essentialist definitions but on subjectivities and coalitions formed across racial, cultural, gendered, and sexual lines.

Although the re-formation of black identity as a concept and the vampire tale and science fiction as genres implies a complete deconstruction of these categories, Gomez and Delany retain some elements of racial identity politics and generic conventions. Both authors create characters that express a form of black or postslave identity somewhat determined by cultural experience. In terms of the popular genres out of which they write, rather than rejecting the vampire tale or science fiction as inferior vehicles of history or creating postmodern parodies of these genres, Gomez and Delany invest them with an ideological project that challenges readers to view the past, present, and future historically. Even as they move farther from the history of slavery and from narrative realism, Gomez and Delany prevent us from dissociating the present and the future from the past. For Gomez, the transhistorical nature of the ageless vampire provides her with an agent of history—a character who is the beneficiary of an expansive historical vision. For Delany, the intergalactic landscape of his text operates as the setting of a technologically advanced world still ravaged by the aftereffects of slavery. This history of slavery does not confine these writers' work or the characters they create. Rather, Gomez and Delany examine the nature of a post-slavery freedom inspired by the slave narratives themselves. They offer us the possibilities of a world at once grounded in the historical and geared toward a future beyond postmodernity.

Historical Agency and the Transhistorical Vampire in Jewelle Gomez's *The Gilda Stories*

The vampire seems an unlikely vehicle through which to engage the historical reality of slavery and its legacy. After all, the vampire is a paradox on a number of levels: neither living nor dead, neither human nor completely inhuman, the vampire as a character seems relegated to a sphere of existence separate from our own. In the context of slavery, however, no paradox seems more significant than the vampire's relationship to time and history. According to the popular mythology, the vampire is, at once, untouched by time and sequestered from human history and the political world. As an archetype, the vampire rejects the historical. In "Recasting the Mythology: Writing Vampire Fiction," Jewelle Gomez outlines her goals in turning to the vampire tale in her fiction and addresses the limitations of this mythology. She states: "The challenge . . . was to create a new mythology, to strip away the dogma that has shaped the vampire figure within the narrow, Western, Caucasian expectation, and to recreate a heroic figure within a broader, more ancient cultural frame of reference" (87–88). On one level, Gomez revises the vampire tale by rejecting the European/ Christian model of the vampire (Bram Stoker's *Dracula* and all his literary and film descendants) in favor of a conception based on Adze, a figure of Ewe mythology and the *kiang-si,* a Chinese mythic figure (87). On another level, Gomez re-forms the vampire tale and the slave narrative by establishing this new mythology within the context of American slavery. Whereas the traditional vampire stands outside history, Gomez's vampires and her protagonist, in particular, are haunted and shaped by history. As such, Gomez mines the transhistorical nature of the vampire. The vampire and the narrative genre as a whole become vehicles of history rather than an escape from it.

Although both the vampire and the vampire tale offer Gomez a means through which to explore slavery across time, the genre, in its traditional form, is in need of re-formation. Even as these texts stretch the culturally inscribed boundaries of decorum by reveling in the overtly violent and sexual threat of vampirism, ultimately they reaffirm a conservative, almost xenophobic agenda. In Bram Stoker's novel *Dracula* (1897), certainly the most enduring and almost omnipresent example of the genre, the corruption of the title character threatens the sexual, national, ethnic purity of the English heroine, Mina. Even as he exists ambiguously on the border between living and dead, between human and inhuman, Dracula is undeniably a foreigner—an outside threat to the conventions of English morality. Dracula's quest to posses Mina, to make her his own, constitutes a supernatural form of miscegenation—the literal mixing of his blood with hers. Although Dracula's vampiric influence and desires taint an already morally ambiguous and susceptible Mina (at least in terms of a patriarchal estimation of her), John Harker and his compatriots successfully avert the foreign corruption by vanquishing the vampire. As a figure, the vampire itself constitutes a threat to be feared and fetishized, in part because of its resemblance to humanity ("Englishness") and its taint of "foreignness."

Although Dracula and other vampire tales appear to disrupt the conventions of realism by delving into the fantastic, most retain the traces, if not the substance, of narrative realism. In its very structure, vampire tales uphold traditional conceptions of "good" and "evil" and of narrative representation.[5] Apart from the vampire itself, these tales follow a linear narrative logic that begins with the threat of the vampire upon the innocent hero or heroine, a period of seduction by the vampire, and finally the reestablishment of order and of good over evil. Even twentieth- and twenty-first-century retellings of the vampire myth like Anne Rice's popular *Interview with the Vampire* retain the conventions popularized by Bram Stoker's novel. Although her vampires are the (often heroic) protagonists of her texts, they also represent the darker, id-like aspects of humanity. In addition, as intricate as their culture and history is, it is entirely separate from human history. Thus, little disruption occurs in the act of reading or viewing these narratives in spite of their rejection of realism in favor of the fantastic. This is particularly true of twenty-first-century readers whose consumption of vampire narratives and whose familiarity with the conventions of the genre isolate the texts themselves from questions of history or narrative realism.

Although *The Gilda Stories* is stylistically conservative (the text follows a linear progression and the presence of vampires does little to disrupt other realistic aspects of the narrative), the context of slavery and the refashioning of the vampire radicalize the genre in oppositional ways. The most significant revision in *The Gilda Stories* is the shift in status of the vampire as "other" in the text. Much as Toni Morrison locates the gothic dimensions of her novel in the slave overseer, schoolteacher, rather than in the supernatural ghost of *Beloved*, Gomez forces us to reconceptualize the threat of violence and the source of evil in the text. As both an escaped slave and a vampire, the protagonist of *The Gilda Stories* (initially referred to as "The Girl") is the hunted rather than the hunter, constantly in danger of discovery and re-enslavement. As such, humans pose the greatest danger in the text. Girl's status as a marginalized other is as much the result of her identity as a former slave, a black woman, and a lesbian as it is the result of her identity as a vampire. Miriam Jones, in her essay "*The Gilda Stories*: Revealing the Monsters at the Margins," points out that the vampires in Gomez's text are disenfranchised primarily on the basis of class, race, ethnic, and sexual difference. Unlike traditional vampires who are predominantly members of the landowning class, most of the vampires of Gomez's text have limited access to economic and cultural power. As her novel projects into a future world, vampires, more than any other group, exist on the margins of society and lie with the threat of enslavement at the hands of the dominant and wealthy culture. In the context of slavery, it would seem most likely that the vampire would correspond to the white, slave owning class. Their exploitation of Africans, the ciphering of their bodies and labor for their own sustenance, constitute a symbolic form of vampirism. Gomez's location of the vampire in the position of the victimized slave constitutes a reordering of the symbolic function of the vampire and a re-formation of the slave/enslaved dichotomy. The distinction between humans and vampires, then, lies not in the act of taking human blood but in the methods and motivations behind that act.

For the vampires in Gomez's novel, taking blood from humans is a nurturing act—a mutually beneficial exchange that operates on a physical, mental, and spiritual level. Gilda, the vampire who transforms the protagonist into a vampire (and whose name "the Girl" ultimately assumes), describes the process of taking blood as a joyful, almost symbiotic act: "We draw life into ourselves yet we give life as well. We give what's needed—energy, dreams, ideas. It's a fair exchange in a world of cheaters" (45).[6] Gomez establishes the oppositional relationship between the degradation of slavery and the symbolic economy of vampirism. Where the former exploits the labor of its victims and ensures the "exchange" by dehumanizing those it enslaves, the latter, in Gomez's re-formation, "humanizes" their victims through the exchange. Gilda's distinction between human violence and vampiric feeding echoes sentiments expressed by the protagonist's mother when asked to explain the actions of her white enslavers. She states: "They ain't been here long 'nough. They just barely human. Maybe not even. They suck up the world, don't taste it" (11). The protagonist's mother proclaims a distinction that not only separates the African slaves from their white oppressors but also anticipates the difference between vampires and humans. Vampires—who engage in a "fair exchange" for blood and whose lives extend through epochs—no longer exist on the border between human and nonhuman. They are, in essence, more human than the white enslavers.

Even before Gomez's protagonist becomes a vampire, the text establishes the connections between her identity as an escaped slave and her future identity as a vampire. The novel begins with the protagonist, who has escaped from a Mississippi plantation and is on the run from a bounty hunter. When she seeks refuge in a farmhouse on the outskirts of New Orleans, the bounty hunter discovers her and begins to rape her. As she reaches for a knife and uses it to defend herself, the language of the text suggests a sensual, vampiric exchange rather than a violent act of self-defense. The description also foreshadows the exchange of blood the protagonist will perform as a vampire:

> He started to enter her, but before his hand finished pulling her open, while it still tingled with the softness of her insides, she entered him with her heart which was now a wood-handled knife. . . . Warmth spread from

his center of power to his chest as the blood left his body. The Girl lay beneath him until her breath became the only sign of life in the pile of hay. She felt the blood draining from him, comfortably warm against her now cool skin. (4)

As an escaped slave, The Girl instinctively turns to a draining of blood that corresponds to the feeding she will perform as a vampire. Where the bounty hunter's penetrative violation is designed to abuse and enslave her, The Girl's penetration of him is an act of resistance and renewal. As his blood spills upon her, she recalls the baths her mother had given her on the plantation. For The Girl, both his blood and her mother's baths physically and spiritually cleanse the abuses of slavery.

When Gilda finds The Girl covered in blood in the farmhouse, she decides to take her into her care. Although initially distrustful of Gilda, a white woman, the stories her mother tells of her Fulani past seem to prepare her for the encounter and for Gilda's powers as a vampire. When she learns of Gilda's ability to read minds, she is startled only by the fact that a white person has the skill. Her gradual acceptance of Gilda as a white woman and a vampire occurs naturally. The community of women she encounters through Gilda at the Woodard house, a brothel Gilda runs, soon becomes a substitute for the family she lost to slavery. A mixture of vampires and humans, of various ethnicities and social stations, the Woodard house represents a safe haven from slavery for the black women who live there and, for the white women who live there, a refuge from the limitations of a patriarchal culture. Although some of the women intuit a difference in Gilda and her partner, Bird, a Lakota woman and also a vampire, none feel threaten by this difference. The Girl establishes a particularly strong bond with Bird who teaches her how to read and to tell stories of her past—a skill that will ultimately allow her to maintain a connection to her cultural history. In constructing this environment, Gomez establishes a pattern of bonding and community building that crosses racial, ethnic, class, and sexual lines.

The allure of a communal identity and the desire to bond with Gilda and Bird more deeply influence The Girl's decision to become a vampire. When Gilda offers her the choice, she cautions her of the price she will pay as a vampire:

What I ask is not an easy thing. You may feel you have nothing to go back to, but sooner or later we all want to go back to something. Usually some inconsequential thing to which we've never given much thought before.

But it will loom there in our past entreating us cruelly because there is no way to ever go back. In asking this of you, and in the future should you ask it of others, you must be certain that you—the others—are strong enough to withstand the complete loss of those intangibles that make the past so alluring. (43)

In many ways, Gilda's conception of life as a vampire recalls the traditional figure of the vampire isolated from the past and from the social world. Although Gilda has established a strong bond and provides a home for the women of the Woodard house, her detachment from history and a broader sense of community causes a crisis of identity. It is this isolation, rather than her identity as a vampire, that leads to her decision to end her life once she has transformed The Girl into a vampire.[7] Gilda's detachment from the past also affects her view of the present. The inevitability of the Civil War represents for her the continuation of human violence rather than a potential end to slavery. She tells The Girl: "Each time I thought slavery or fanaticism could be banished from the earth with a law or a battle. Each time I've been wrong. I've run out of youthful caring" (45). Unlike Gilda, her partner, Bird, maintains a link to her Lakota history and her past through storytelling and by periodically returning to her people. Clearly it is a choice Gilda has made to isolate herself from her past life rather than an inevitable result of existing as a vampire. In fact, as The Girl learns after her own transformation, the vampire must maintain some connection to its personal past. By carrying the soil of one's homeland, a vampire can protect herself from the lethal effects of the sun. Although Gilda maintains this practice herself, she ultimately relinquishes it to kill herself by swimming out to sea in the sunlight.

The Girl's transformation into a vampire at the end of the first chapter marks the beginning of her post-slave identity as Gilda. Although the rest of the novel follows her life after slavery has ended, Gomez, like Reed, Butler, and other writers of the postmodern slave narrative, emphasizes the interrelated nature of past and present and establishes the history of slavery as the foundation of Gilda's later experiences. Gilda spends her life as a part of multiple communities, both vampire and human, very much a part of the social movements through history. Her participation in a women's social group in Missouri in 1921, her involvement with a theatre group in New York during the Black Arts movement, her life as a jazz singer in the 1980s, all contain the traces of her earlier life not as a vampire but as a human. In each of these roles, Gilda passes for human and retains her identity as a black woman, establishing bonds with other black women.

Although her identity as a vampire separates her in some way, she takes "comfort in their familiar smells and sounds and the rare sense of unity that sometimes crept into her" (112). More than just episodes of history, Gilda's travels across the country reflect the continuance of her multifaceted identity and her historical agency. Like *Kindred*'s Dana Franklin, Gilda, as the beneficiary of a historical vision, often draws parallels to and makes connections between events in the present (the rampant lynching in the first decades of the twentieth century, the Attica uprising in 1971) and slavery.

As Gilda develops these human bonds she also maintains her vampire family and creates new bonds with other vampires. When she reluctantly leaves the Woodard house and travels to Yerba Buena in 1890, she establishes a bond with Sorel and Anthony, two white gay male vampires who were associates of the original Gilda. Through them she learns more about herself as a vampire and about the larger community of vampires, including the division between those who seek a symbiotic relationship with humans and those rare vampires who cultivate a more antagonistic and violent relationship. Gilda's relationship with Bird also continues to grow in spite of the time they often spend apart when Bird travels and visits her people. In constructing these relationships in conjunction with her human connections, Gilda creates a multifaceted subjectivity that incorporates her cultural identity with a commitment to communities built across racial, gendered, and class lines. The human and vampire communities occasionally intersect, particularly in the rare instances when Gilda contemplates turning a human into a vampire. Her long-standing reluctance to bring someone into her vampire family comes not as a result of a sense of exclusivity but because of her unwillingness to create a union that is not mutually beneficial to all involved. When she finally decides to bring in additional members of the vampire community (first Julius, a young black man she meets in 1971, and later Effie, who is already a vampire) she broadens her coalition based on this mutual exchange.

Even as Gomez constructs an idealized vampire communal ethic as an alternative to the fractured human community, she tempers this utopian vision by returning to the echoes of slavery. In the final chapter of the novel, the year is 2050 and the planet is suffering from an environmental crisis that causes disease and famine. Many wealthy humans have left Earth, but those who remain hire bounty hunters to capture and enslave vampires. The vampire's power of granting immortality comes at a high price. Some even work in league with humans to enslave other vampires. One of the last vampires of her family to remain in North America, Gilda must, once again, escape enslavement, this time by moving south to Machu Picchu. The final image of the novel is of Gilda watching the last members of her family moving parallel to her across the distance, on their way to the same destination. With this image, Gomez retains a positive vision of vampirism even as her narrative arrives full circle with a return to slavery. The coalition of vampires at the end of the novel suggests the possibility, the necessity, even, of constructing bonds across lines as a means of survival. In spite of the renewed threat of slavery, the basis of the optimism at the end of the novel lies in Gilda's history of survival and her transhistorical knowledge that freedom is possible even if it is always already contested.

The circular structure of Gomez's vampiric slave narrative reinforces the historical dimensions of her text and its examination of slavery. As much as she defamiliarizes the slave experience through the revised mythology of the vampire, the incorporation of the fantastic constitutes a reinvestment in historical agency. The narrative movement in time from the history of slavery, to its legacy in the present and into a speculative future requires a historical vision—one that re-forms the past in order to project a future.

Stars in My Pocket like Grains of Sand and the Interstellar Slave Narrative

Samuel Delany's *Stars in My Pocket like Grains of Sand* engages in a similar merger of past, present, and future as *The Gilda Stories*. In place of the transhistorical vampire, Delany mines the expansive spatial and temporal landscape of science fiction. This genre allows him to address the complexities of achieving an identity after slavery, the postmodern challenges of living amidst competing cultures, institutions, and systems of knowledge; and the potentially dehumanizing effects of advancing technologies. Where historical realism as a narrative mode confines itself to the past as the site of history, the concept of the past, present, and future as sites of history occupies a familiar place in science fiction. Unlike other postmodern slave narratives I have discussed, Delany projects the history of slavery into a completely fictional world. As such, *Stars* is the most removed and "alien" of these narratives. However, even in its futuristic depiction, *Stars* establishes a link between the condition of slavery and the present.

The union of the historical with the futuristic elements of science fiction characterizes much of Delany's work throughout his long career as a science fiction writer. As Teresa De Lauretis points out, Delany's science fiction, in spite of its rejection of traditional, linear progression, remains fundamentally historical. History becomes "a discontinuous series of multiple intersecting signs, a discursive construction of reality at once subjective and objective" (173). Robert Elliot Fox also notes the importance of history as a fundamental component of Delany's work. However, Fox suggests that it is the familiar and repetitive quality of history that allows science fiction to evoke the past, present, and future from an historical perspective. If history is ultimately ever unfolding, Fox argues that "in going forward, it may only be recovering the same ground: a circular movement of ever unsatisfied desire" (99). In many ways, Delany's treatment of slavery is a fusion of these two views of time and history. *Stars* achieves authority over the past by both retaining and resolving a central paradox in the narrative representation of the future as history. On one hand, Delany retains the postmodernist view of history as an always already subjective (and therefore fallible) reconstruction of the past. The very nature of language itself and our inability to access the past directly render the past (and the representation of it) unstable and multiple. On the other hand, Delany's circular conception of time renders the past knowable in its very repeatability. A futuristic vision, in these terms, becomes a historical one if it reveals the circular pattern at work. As readers, then, we must establish the authority of Delany's text by mapping this pattern as it manifests itself in its treatment of slavery.

Delany's conditional authority as well as his complex treatment of language, power, and identity reflects his interest in post-structuralism. Just as narrative history is always unstable, always contested, for Delany, identity itself is the product of diverse forces (including language and structures of meaning) that pre-exist it. This view of identity places him, perhaps more than any other writer I have discussed so far, on the border between African American and Eurocentric postmodernism. This proximity defamiliarizes his re-formation of slavery in complicated ways.[8] Like Charles Johnson, Delany resists the tendency to essentialize racial identity. The racial identity of the protagonist in *Stars*, although meant to evoke connections with those who suffered under the Atlantic slave trade, is unspecified. In addition, Delany further destabilizes racial identity by portraying a vast and complex social system made up of multiple species and cultures in his novel. However, rather than avoiding or obscuring questions of ideology, Delany focuses on the ideological foundations of identity and its impact on his work. In the afterword written for the 1990 reprinting of *Stars*, Delany states that one of his goals as a writer is to dismantle persistent ideologies that suppress the free play of difference:

I think that anytime when there was such a notion of a centered subject, especially when related to the white, western, patriarchal nuclear family, not only was it an ideological mirage, it was a mirage that necessarily grew up to mask the psychological, economic, and material oppression of an 'other.' . . . And I feel that the times and places where the 'fragmented subject' is at its healthiest, happiest, and most creative is precisely at those times where society and economics contrive (1) to make questions of unity and centeredness irrelevant, and (2) to distance that subject as much as possible from such oppressions. (384)

Delany rejects the essentialism of both white Western patriarchy and, by implication, black cultural nationalism and posits another ideology of subjectivity in its place: an ideology of fragmentation. But, in establishing this fragmentation within the context of slavery as he does in *Stars,* Delany locates rather than obscures its source; fragmentation is both a product of and an ideological response to slavery. Part of his project is to draw parallels between the contemporary struggle for identity amidst cultural multiplicity and alienation with his protagonist's quest as a survivor of slavery in a futuristic and alien culture. In essence, the novel posits the interstellar as the metaphor for the global. The prospect of creating an interstellar identity produces new anxieties, as cohesion seems even more complex under these circumstances. Although the signs of power and ideology are multiple, complex, and dispersed across an intergalactic setting, like other postmodern slave narratives, *Stars* returns to the history of slavery in order to interrogate its devastating impact on individual and cultural identity.

From the outset of the novel, Delany fuses the past, present, and future by depicting a system of slavery that not only resembles our postmodern condition but also surpasses it as a result of the advancements in science and technology. With the circular nature of time implicit in Delany's work, readers must confront the horrific possibility that the legacy of slavery will not only persist in the future but also will render its practices more efficiently. The main character, Korga, inhabits the distant planet Rhyonon and faces the prospect of living as a slave. Only a young man, he has led a life of crime and violence and has been ostracized by the dominant culture for his physical size and appearance, his sexual preference for other men, and his inability to learn proficiently. According to authorities, his marginalized status on Rhyonon produces an anxiety that finds expression only in criminal behavior and a sense of social alienation. Korga contemplates submission to a process called Radical Anxiety Termination (RAT) that will eradicate the brain functions responsible for his socially disruptive behavior. As officials from the RAT Institute tell him: "Of course . . . you will be a slave . . . but you will be happy . . . certainly you will be happier than you are"(3). The process will cure him of his propensity toward violence, criminality, and drug use, thereby allowing him to fit into society more effectively. In a state of confusion and with little comprehension of the ramifications of his decision, Korga hesitantly submits to the RAT technique. The process of alienating Korga from his own identity occurs instantaneously—the essence of self is confined to specific areas of the brain and eradicated. What took generations under American slavery, the Institute accomplishes in seconds. Unlike the Atlantic slave trade, which systematically ripped Africans from their homeland and dehumanized them through protracted physical and mental abuse, radical anxiety termination strips Korga, now known as Rat Korga, of his own subjectivity through a sanitized and invisible procedure. He loses not only the means to resist his enslavement but also the ability to comprehend his own status as a slave. The process creates a shell of a man, a commodity bought and sold against his will, easily subjugated by those who exploit his labor.

Under the guise of paternalistic benevolence, the Institute uses the RAT process as a means of maintaining social order. Korga believes that the Institute represents the only way to overcome his alienation and become a part of the society that has devalued him. Behind the benevolent facade of curing his "uncivilized" behavior, however, the Institute obscures the real purpose of the RAT process. The Institute seeks to use the technique to transform Korga into a subhuman commodity and to exploit him as slave labor. Much like American slavery, which justified the enslavement and abuse of Africans through a discourse rooted in Christianity and democracy, the Institute characterizes Korga's mental subjugation and physical enslavement as both personally and socially beneficial. According to the narrative the Institute constructs, industrial slavery and the RAT process create a happy existence that will halt Korga's destructive and misguided impulses even as it brings economic prosperity to the Institute as an organization.

The technology of slavery in this distant and remote future has also expanded beyond the individual ownership of human subjects into the corporate ownership of slaves. In the "advanced" economic structure of Rhyonon, slavery has literally and figuratively masked itself behind the faceless corporation as the organizing institution of oppression. It is now illegal for individuals to own slaves. As a result, the slave labor force becomes an invisible part of the political economy. In turn, members of the dominant class wear masks in order to obscure themselves from the view of those they enslave. Unlike the American system of slavery in which the individual slave owner is immediately recognizable to the slave as the source of oppression, Rhyonon's corporate institution of slavery conceals both the slave and the enslaver in the vast exchange of human commodities. The RAT Institute buys and sells those it enslaves with little regard for either the slaves it creates or the private companies that purchase the slaves as labor. Much as Ishmael Reed uses material anachronism to locate the legacy of slavery in commodity culture, Delany uses the conventions of science fiction to assert that the diffusion of power in technologically and economically advanced cultures continues to exploit racial and ethnic minorities and has its origins in slavery. However, resistance to this form of advanced enslavement is more difficult to locate.

In spite of Rhyonon's conversion of the slave into an industrial commodity, the institution of slavery still has broader cultural implications. Korga's status as a slave increases his value on the free market. Eventually, he is sold illegally to a woman as a sex slave. Although she provides him with a momentary, yet monumental, respite from his physical subjugation, it remains another, more individualized form of exploitation. Although allowing slaves to read is illegal, the woman, in an effort to increase his value to her, gives him a mechanical glove that bypasses the synaptic damage done by the RAT process. The glove grants Korga access to written language that, in turn, allows him to gain knowledge of his world and his culture. Within hours, he consumes dozens of texts written over the course of his world's history.[9] The narrator describes the moment Korga regains his intellectual and subjective consciousness when he first wears the glove:

> All sensations, as well as the faintest memories associated with them, were given a word and three written versions of it. . . . The new condition was not so much an alternate voice loud enough to drown out the voices of childhood as it was a web, a text weaving endlessly about him, erupting into and falling from consciousness, prompting memory and obliterating it. (37)

The moment Korga acquires the ability to understand the language of his oppressors recalls the moment when Frederick Douglass learns the importance of reading the English language in his 1845 *Narrative*. For enslaved African Americans like Douglass, the ability to read represented the ability to construct an independent and liberating sense of identity. Frederick Douglass describes his experience as one of revelation—the essence of an emergent consciousness: "It was a new and special revelation, explaining dark and mysterious things, with which my youthful understanding had struggled, but struggled in vain. It was a grand achievement and I prized it highly. From that moment, I understood the pathway from slavery to freedom" (Gates 275). Just as the technologies of slavery have advanced, the pathway to freedom is equally advanced. Korga, almost instantaneously, gains access to a world denied him by the RAT process and by his enslavement to the Institute.

His access to cultural and textual information proves to be short-lived, however, when the authorities of the Institute capture the woman who owns him and reclaim possession of their stolen commodity. When they find Korga, the authorities rip the mechanical glove from his hand and thus violently sever him from his only access to a sense of knowledge and individual identity. Just as the ability to read gave Korga a sense of the world around him and the cultural history of which he was a part, its absence leaves him with a feeling of profound loss and the sensation of having his identity ripped away:

> Qualitatively, the feeling was somewhat like being in the midst of an involuted argument with a particularly complex point to make, only to open your mouth and forget what you were about to say. Quantitatively, it was so much more intense than simple forgetting that anyone who'd undergone the experience would probably question the qualitative as a metaphor to convey the quantity of that shattering erasure. For what had been stripped, wrenched, excised from him at that tug was all in him that could have understood the very description of it. Left was only a tingling that worked through every cell of him. (57)

Re-enslavement results in not only a denial of freedom but also a loss of self and a relinquishing of consciousness. With the illusion of freedom severed, Korga must return to his hollow life as a slave. Both the prologue and Korga's re-enslavement end abruptly. Shortly after his recapture, Korga's world is destroyed as a result of civil war. Rhyonon has experienced "Cultural Fugue"—the inability to resolve the multiple and conflicting ideologies at work in the culture. The rest of the novel examines Korga's search for a post-slavery identity on a new and alien world as the sole survivor of the war.

The second section of the novel, "Monologues: Visible and Invisible Persons Distributed in Space," focuses on the relationship between Korga and Marq Dyeth, an Industrial Diplomat from the planet Velm. Due to their potential attraction to each other, the two men are thrust together by the Web, an interstellar organization that controls the system of languages, information, and cultural protocols for hundreds of worlds. Korga must achieve a sense of identity and home on Velm through his relationship with his perfect erotic object, Marq Dyeth, who, in turn, must facilitate Korga's assimilation into this alien culture. In placing Rat Korga on Velm, the Web places him in a complex culture that struggles with its own diversity. Far from a utopian world, Delany constructs Velm as a complex and problematic society struggling with the challenges of cultural and sexual difference. Velm is inhabited by two species: the evelmi, dragonlike creatures indigenous to the planet, and the humans, who colonized the world several centuries before the time of the narrative. On the surface, relations between the humans and the evelmi are strong and productive; members of both species often occupy the same family and pursue sexual unions with one another. The interaction between the two species occurs successfully in the southern region of the planet where Marq Dyeth and his ancestors have always resided. However, in the northern region of the planet, relations between humans and evelmi are tentative, at best, with frequent acts of violence, hostility, and economic disparity occurring between them.

In order to assist Korga in his quest, the Web reverses the damage done by the RAT process by linking him to the General Information system (GI), which allows his brain to process information. This system links all sentient beings to a centralized source that provides information on the multiple cultures and species that make up the Web. Unable to counteract the RAT technique completely, the Web discovers that the only way to provide Korga access to any information is to give him a set of mechanized rings. Much like the mechanical glove of the Prologue (though far less efficient), Korga must wear the rings in order to process information about the world around him. Although the Web successfully "remaps the survivor" by giving him the tools to think and learn again, Korga cannot receive information directly from GI and, therefore, processes information about cultural difference much more slowly than other inhabitants of Velm. In addition, Korga receives information provided by the Web, a governing agency and a mechanism of power. Korga has the means to process information the Web provides, but he is still unable to construct his own knowledge and his own sense of history. Ultimately this limitation undermines his ability to find his own identity and to consider Velm his home.

The problems of cultural difference on Velm clearly reflect our own. Just as the advanced technology of the RAT process demonstrates the increased ability to enslave individuals in the future, the intercultural complexities of different species occupying the same social space marks a similar "advancement" in the sociocultural realm. Advancement in this context, however, does not signify a transcendence of racial hierarchies and oppression; rather, it reflects the increased mechanics of "othering" in the future. Delany replaces the distinctions we make on subtle differences in physical characteristics and cultural practices with the vast differences between species. Distinctions of skin color have been overshadowed by the fact that humans must share the same space with the evelmi who have six legs, several tongues, wings, and three sexes: male, female, and neuter. Difference lies well beyond issues of social structure, language, and culture and manifests itself on the level of biology. As such, the potential for discrimination and systematic oppression remains ever present, unchanged by the various advancements in science and technology.

The tensions of difference on Velm are a microcosm of the six thousand worlds that make up the community of planets in the novel. What unites these sometimes competing and conflicting worlds, however, is the prevailing fear of Cultural Fugue. In Delany's apocalyptic vision, Cultural Fugue is the literal self-destruction of a world due to the inhabitants' inability to handle difference and socioeconomic conflict.[10] The vast array of species and cultures, histories, and organizing systems of government represents the potential source of destruction for each planet. And yet, the conflicting ideologies espoused by the two agencies which govern most of the six thousand worlds, the Family and the Sygn, perhaps play an even greater role in both provoking and preventing this phenomenon. The function of these two governing agencies is to deal with the shifting pluralities that often precipitate the self-destruction of worlds.[11] According to Marq Dyeth, the Family attempts to achieve cultural stability by "trying to establish the dream of a classic past as pictured on a world that may never even have existed" (87). It is a conservative and monocultural worldview that subverts multiplicity, undermining its presence by maintaining racial (or "specieal" in intergalactic terms), social, and gender hierarchies. In contrast, the Sygn seeks to establish cultural cohesion in the face of multiplicity by committing itself to "the living interaction and difference between each woman and each world from which the right stability and play may flower" (87). The Sygn worldview is the essence of multiculturalism and focuses on the free play of difference as a means of preventing Cultural Fugue.[12] Each planet must choose one of these worldviews as its organizing agency, yet the process of making this choice often leaves the world most vulnerable to destruction. Rhyonon, Korga's homeworld, was destroyed during a period of political struggle between two factions, each wanting to align itself with an opposing agency.

In spite of the relative freedom and promotion of pluralism on Velm, the cultural cohesion of the world is still a work in progress. In fact, one could argue that the Sygn system's emphasis on pluralism itself poses its own critical problems for Korga's quest for identity. As the sole survivor of Rhyonon—a world that had stripped him of his cultural history and language—Korga must achieve a sense of self from the fragments of its destruction. Without a coherent sense of his own identity, Korga must assimilate into a culture of multiple identities, each struggling to maintain a sense of its history while living cohesively with one another. The Sygn, as a governing agency, promotes this struggle in an effort to establish a pluralistic culture that benefits from diversity. But, as Marq Dyeth describes it, a crucial component of the Sygn ideology, the cultural mechanism that holds the society in place, is the interwoven links between history, home, and identity:

> The Sygn is concerned with preserving the history of local spaces . . . but one of the Sygn's most widely spread tenets . . . is that history is what is outside, in both time and space, the current moment of home. And without history, there is no home. A second tenet that usually . . . goes along with the first: when you go to a new world, all you can take of your home is its history. And if you are a woman, your choice is to take it knowingly and be its (and your new home's) silent friend, or to take it unknowingly and be its (and your new home's) loud slave. (104)

Across the Velmian landscapes are sites of cultural identity, repositories of history that mark the past and give both human and evelmi a sense of home. For Korga, Velm offers no sense of self, no markers of history or heritage that would allow him to feel a sense of home. Korga's estrangement reaches beyond the experience of those ripped from their African homeland who can reconstruct their lost heritage through the persistent traces left in oral and cultural traditions. Instead, Korga's home and history, first in his enslavement to the RAT Institute and ultimately in the destruction of his homeland, have been eradicated. He is a diaspora of one—disconnected from his homeland and from Velm as the outsider with no home, no history, and no identity. He remains history's (and Velm's) "loud slave," subjugated by his own alienation much as he has been on Rhyonon.

The Web, in placing Korga in the care of Marq Dyeth, tries to counteract Korga's sense of social alienation through the liaison with his perfect erotic object. The Web believes that the sexual connection between the two men will allow Korga to transcend the cultural difference that marks him as alien/other. As such, the sexual union represents a means by which Korga can gain a sense of home and replace his lack of a cultural history. When Korga finally arrives on Velm, he meets Dyeth and the two begin a brief but powerful union. Marq, as an official representative to interstellar travelers, is in a unique position to introduce Korga to the various cultures and histories of the planet. Over the course of a day, Marq and Korga explore their sexual relationship and interact with the various inhabitants of the planet, both human and evelmi. Initially, Korga's introduction to the planet seems successful; the rings of Vondramach Orr allow him to process the information Marq relates to him about human and evelmi culture. But soon it becomes obvious that his status as the sole survivor of a planet destroyed by Cultural Fugue marks him as distinctly different from the inhabitants of Velm.

Korga's presence on Velm seems more beneficial to the world's inhabitants than it is to him as an individual. On Rhyonon, Korga was a physical commodity, but on Velm he has become a cultural commodity—valuable only in his difference from the dominant culture. This difference gives Korga consumable use value, but ultimately constrains his individual identity. Korga represents what evelmi and humans on Velm are not: the lone survivor of a distant world. Humans and evelmi seek Korga out, trying to possess him in some intangible way, sometimes sexually, sometimes intellectually, because of the knowledge his survival has brought him. His status as "other" only increases his existential alienation and undermines his quest for identity. As such, Korga is both seen and unseen by those he encounters on Velm, visible in his alien difference but invisible in everyone's inability to comprehend his marginalized identity. In a conversation with Marq, Korga describes his feelings of estrangement even on a world so intent on embracing his presence: "On my world . . . it was always assumed there was nothing about me to know. Here everyone seems to know everything. I don't know—perhaps it is the GI they can't connect me with. But the feeling, Marq, . . . is much the same" (253). Korga is the subject of knowledge, subjugated by its traces across the General Information system. As humans and evelmi seek him out, they categorize him as "other"—a mirror reflection of their own susceptibility to Cultural Fugue. But Korga also represents the possibility of survival in the face of their greatest fear: apocalypse. And when someone asks him what it feels like to have lost an entire world, Korga responds: "Lonely. . . . But the loneliness comes from the question. . . . 'What is it like to lose a world?' is the first question everyone who meets me asks; so I am alone with my own feelings, sights, sounds, and experiences, which can only provide answer to the question: What is it like to be presented with a new one?" (293).

Even as Marq tries to shield Korga from those who seek him out, he, too, cannot fully understand Korga's position as outsider on Velm. In spite of their sexual compatibility and the potential for a romantic liaison, cohesion between the two men does not occur easily. Marq, as a member of the Dyeth "stream"—a family unit based not on biological connections between members but on the social and child-rearing connections between both humans and evelmi—has access to a wealth of information on his "stream's" history.[13] Gylda Dyeth, as a powerful figure in Velm history, has given her descendants an influential class status on the world, an ancestral mansion, and a wealth of historical documents written by and about her. Unlike Marq, who maintains a strong link to his family heritage as a descendent of Gylda Dyeth and who has lived on a world that has promoted cultural diversity and "interspeceial" interaction, Korga's has no historical or cultural context to his existence. His only cultural experience has been on a world that oppressed him because of his physical and sexual difference and that erased all traces of his history. As we saw in Octavia Butler's *Kindred,* Dana and Kevin Franklin's interracial relationship is marked by a similar discrepancy. Dana's only knowledge of her ancestors comes as a result of her time travel. In the present, her ancestors are obscured by the absence of historical records. For Korga, as for Dana, there is no mythical or ancestral home to which he can return—no oral or written histories which will give him access to all that he has lost.

The cultural difference between Marq and Korga becomes fully apparent during a formal dinner at Dyethshome. Held in honor of both Korga and the Thants, long-standing friends of Marq's family, the dinner illustrates on a number of levels the reality that neither Korga nor the inhabitants of Velm can fully transcend their cultural differences through sexual union. The Thants, a family solely made up of humans, have relocated to a world governed by the Family and, as a result, have rejected the Sygn principles which form the basis of Velm culture. When members of the Thants criticize Marq and the other human members of his family for their sexual interactions with the evelmi (whom the Thants consider animals), this reflects the ideology of the Family system and recalls the ideologies that lie behind antimiscegenation laws and the continuing conflicts surrounding interracial relationships in contemporary culture. Marq, insulted by the Thants' criticism, describes his reaction to Korga, stating: "they made me feel as if I were living on some world out of history where all that we do here was against the law"(337). Rat points out that Marq cannot feel this way because he has no personal access to that experience. He responds: "They didn't make you feel that way. That's the way they made me feel. You didn't grow up on such a world. You didn't spend your childhood and make your transition to maturity on a world where bestiality and homosexuality were legally proscribed. So you do not possess the fund of those feelings to draw on. I do" (337). To some extent, Korga can identify with the Thants in a way that he cannot identify with Marq. As he puts it, "they [the Thants] come from such a world. Otherwise, it would never have occurred to them to say such things" (337). For Korga, it is an important distinction between imagining a cultural experience and living that experience. Korga argues that one cannot imagine an identity into being but can only create one out of the elements of one's own experience, history, and heritage. The Thants' worldview is similar to the worldview on Rhyonon that persecuted and alienated Korga because his identity did not conform to the accepted and organizing principles of the dominant culture. It is a similar world view to our own—an ideology governed by the norms and values of a dominant and dominating Eurocentric culture.

Korga and Marq cannot fully transcend the differences between them, though their romantic connection does afford them a state of mutual acceptance. However, Korga's presence on Velm as a whole proves much more difficult to negotiate. As his time on the world increases by only a matter of hours, thousands of people, human and evelmi, clamor to see him, threatening to overtake Dyethshome. Korga's presence brings Velm to the brink of Cultural Fugue. The situation forces the Web to take Korga away from Velm, leaving Marq feeling abandoned and alone. In the end, he must return to his profession as an Industrial Diplomat and Korga must continue his search for a home elsewhere.

The Epilogue of the novel focuses on Marq's life after Korga has been taken from Velm. As a result of their brief relationship, Marq has come to view his own subjectivity differently. In light of his profession as an interstellar Industrial Diplomat, his experience with Korga forces Marq to draw parallels between his own subject position as an outsider to the worlds he visits and the fragmented nature of his own identity as other when he is away from home. Though Marq can always return to his home to recover his sense of place and identity, he realizes that the ability to maintain a coherent and unified sense of self in the face of multiplicity is a constant struggle. Marq can begin to approximate an understanding of Korga's subject position through an understanding of his own. He states:

To leave one part of the world in order to visit another is to indulge in a transformation of signs, their appearances, their meanings, that, however violent, still, because of the coherence of the transformative system itself, partakes of a logic, a purely geographical order, if not the more entailed connections lent by ecological or social factors: here they do it one way, there they do it another—with no doubt as to the identity of the antecedents of both 'its.' But to leave a world, and to leave it at dawn . . . is to experience precisely the problematics of that identity at its most intense: to see that identity shatter, fragment, and to realize that its solidity was always an illusion, and that infinite spaces between those referential shards are more opaque to direct human apprehension than all the star-flooded vacuum. (364)

It is on this open-ended note that Delany concludes his novel, the first in a projected diptych that he plans to resolve in the yet unwritten novel, *The Splendor and Misery of Bodies, of Cities.* We can only speculate on the nature of Korga's continuing quest for a sense of self and home in the face of his estrangement from his cultural history. Delany also leaves it unclear to what extent Marq and Korga can bridge their differences in order to achieve a stable, romantic relationship. Even in an inherently speculative genre such as science fiction, it is difficult (and perhaps undesirable) to project a world that transcends the fundamental limitations of our own— to project an alternative to that which has governed our lives for so long. In the novel's open-endedness, Delany does not provide us with a utopian vision of our contemporary moment, but rather posits a critique of the oppressive legacies of slavery that threaten to persist into the distant future. Delany does imply that Korga's quest for identity in the face of cultural difference and the legacy of slavery is an ongoing one that reaches back into our past histories, our present circumstances, and into our future existence.

That both Delany and Gomez examine the quest for identity through slavery and its legacy in contemporary American culture clearly aligns their texts with other African American postmodern slave narratives. However, in their projection of future worlds marked by cultural fragmentation, commodity culture, racism, and alienation, Delany and Gomez push the circular nature of the postmodern slave narrative one step further. Even as they project the legacy of slavery into the future, Delany and Gomez project our contemporary postmodernist culture there as well. As a result, their exploration of the post-slavery identity is a narrative representation of our postmodern selves.

conclusion

T HE constellation of texts that I define as postmodern slave narratives is, as we have seen, complex and diverse. From the parodic and satirical treatment of slavery in Ishmael Reed's *Flight to Canada* to Toni Morrison's haunting and melancholic treatment in *Beloved,* the African American postmodern slave narrative encompasses a wide range of aesthetic and political responses to the history of American slavery and its continuing legacy. The purpose of my project has been to examine these varying and often conflicted responses while simultaneously theorizing the common foundation these texts share. Rather than an all encompassing, stable genre, the African American postmodern slave narrative, much like "white" postmodern historical fictions, reflects a common need to critique the truth claims of objectivity and authenticity embedded in traditional history and narrative realism. How black writers have responded to this need varies from the inflections of black feminist thought and the implied claims of narrative authority in Butler's *Kindred* and Morrison's *Beloved* to the rejection of such claims in Charles Johnson's metafictional narrative *Oxherding Tale.* Ultimately, African American postmodernism in general, and the postmodern slave narrative more specifically, is a complex discourse united by a commitment to re-forming the past through narrative.

The postmodern slave narrative is transgressive. It blurs the boundaries between genres, crossing them relentlessly and reinvesting popular forms often regarded as escapist or ahistorical with an overtly political dimension. It deconstructs realism as the dominant mode of historical narrative even as (in many instances) it implies that the past history of slavery is a knowable object, retrievable through written form. It merges the conflicting discourses of postmodernism, black cultural nationalism, and black feminism, complicating each in the process. It conceptualizes black subjectivity and racial identity, in its past and present incarnations, in a complex manner that simultaneously rejects essentialism but acknowledges the need to create communities based on a shared history and culture. In the novels by Gomez and Delany, in particular, the postmodern slave narrative acknowledges the need to forge identities and communities beyond these racial categories in order to achieve liberation in a postmodern context. But, in spite of these transgressive tendencies, or perhaps because of them, writers of the postmodern slave narrative, much like their nineteenth-century counterparts, exhibit a persistent faith in the liberating potential of narrative fiction. For these writers, the act of re-forming the past is an overtly political gesture—a means of critiquing the legacy of slavery in the present by radicalizing our view of the past.

An implicit argument in my reading of the postmodern slave narrative as a transgressive form is that these texts, written in a span of sixteen years (1976–1991), constitute an epoch of sorts within the African American literary response to the history of slavery. Much as Georg Lukacs in *The Historical Novel* argues that the classical historical novel (as exemplified by the novels of Sir Walter Scott) arose out of a rising class consciousness as a result of the French Revolution, one could argue that the postmodern slave narrative is also the product of a distinct cultural moment in history. With the waning of the promise of both the civil rights movement of the 1960s and the radical politics of black cultural nationalism in the late sixties and early seventies, black writers sought a new literary form that would retain elements of these discourses while also responding to the developing discourse of postmodernism. For Lukacs, the classical historical novel arose out of the developing sense of history as having a direct effect on the life of every individual (as opposed to just the bourgeois or royal classes). As a result, texts produced in Europe during the late eighteenth century, for the first time, brought "the past to life as the prehistory of the present" (*Historical* 52).[1] Similarly, the African American postmodern slave narrative's return to the history of slavery reflected a developing sense that the cultural politics of the Reagan-Bush years was an extension of the past. During a time when blacks continued to struggle with poverty, unemployment, and homelessness in increasingly disproportionate numbers, these texts represented the strategic reclamation and articulation of a liberating identity for the postmodern age.

My reference to Lukacs in conjunction with the postmodern slave narrative may seem somewhat ironic given the fact that he viewed realism as the most effective and potentially liberating mode of historical fiction. For Lukacs, anti-realist movements like Expressionism, Surrealism, and Modernism alienated readers from a sense of history by retreating into a subjective and solipsistic emphasis on the present.[2] He argues: "A campaign against realism, whether conscious or not, and a resultant impoverishment and isolation of literature and art is one of the crucial manifestations of decadence in the realm of art" ("Realism" 1057). And yet, postmodern slave narratives retain many of the goals Lukacs lays out for historical fiction. These novels promote an active engagement with the past as a totality—one that reveals a continuing history of racial oppression and economic exploitation. Where writers of the postmodern slave narrative diverge from Lukacs's formulation is their insistence that realism and its conventions are no longer the most effective means to engage and reclaim that history. In their use of the fantastic and their rejection of realism, writers of the postmodern slave narrative revitalize our engagement with historical reality and force us to contemplate how narrative discourse (both fantastic and realist) shapes our experience of it.

In following Lukacs's example and characterizing the postmodern slave narrative as a distinct epoch in historical fiction, the question arises: Has there been a shift away from the formal choices and ideological implications of the postmodern slave narrative? With the popular and critical success of texts like Edward P. Jones's Pulitzer prize-winning novel *The Known World* (2003) and Steven Barnes's historical romance and alternate history *Lion's Blood* (2002), there is little question that the resonance of slavery in the literary imagination of readers and writers persists. Given the profound impact the legacy of slavery still has on contemporary racial politics, economic conditions, and cultural attitudes, it should come as no surprise that black writers continue to return to this moment in history. Although it would be an oversimplification to suggest that there has been a radical break from the generic innovations of the postmodern slave narrative, I would argue that an examination of these two texts reveal a retreat from the transgressive dimensions of the novels in this study. Although both *The Known World* and *Lion's Blood* bear the traces of influence of the postmodern slave narratives I have discussed, each maintains some distinction between realism and fantasy as narrative modes of representing the past. Rather than blurring the boundaries between genres, Jones complicates the history of slavery within the bounds of realism while Barnes re-examines the past from within the realm of fantastic literature.

In *The Known World*, Edward P. Jones examines a dimension of American slavery often ignored in both historical and fictional accounts:

the communities of free blacks who owned slaves. Much as Morrison tells the stories of the slaves and their interior lives obscured by traditional history in *Beloved*, Jones complicates our understanding of what have become almost archetypal figures in American literature: the enslaver and the slave. Although his transformation of these figures is less radical than what we see in Charles Johnson's work, Jones forces us to embrace a more complex view of slavery as a social system rather than merely an economic one. By creating characters like Henry Townsend, the black slave owner, and John Skiffington, the conflicted white sheriff who abhors slavery but upholds the slave laws of the South, Jones suggests that a narrow view of the past ultimately leads to a limited conception of race, intraracial relationships, and interracial relationships.[3]

Like several writers of postmodern slave narratives, Jones posits traditional history and the official historical record (characterized in the form of census takers, historians, and pamphleteers) against the more open-ended, oral, and speculative narrative style of the narrator. Anderson Frazier, a minor but recurring character in the novel, is a white Canadian pamphlet writer who interviews Fern Elston, a black slave owner. The narrator consistently points out all the information Fern omits in her interviews with him, thus highlighting the fissures that occur in historical accounts. The narrator also refers to the mistakes census takers made, often out of willful ignorance and racist attitudes, that ultimately undermine the accuracy of the official historical record. In their place, the omniscient narrator brings to bear on the story a vast knowledge drawn from oral accounts, interior monologues, extended dream sequences, and, perhaps most important, a view of time that spans generations. These elements work together to form a tapestry of narrative realism that acknowledges the relationship between past and present. The novel presents the passage of time as a continuum rather than conflating time periods. Although Jones does incorporate some elements of the fantastic and magical realism in his narrative (most notably in dream sequences), the novel does not draw overtly from other genres and non-mimetic forms. Rather, he uses the convention of the omniscient third-person narrator to broaden the scope of historical realism beyond the limitations of the official historical record. As such, *The Known World* revises rather than re-forms our understanding of slavery.

Where Jones expands the parameters of historical realism by manipulating the existing conventions of the genre, Steven Barnes infuses his essentially fantastic narrative with echoes of the real. In *Lion's Blood*, Barnes creates an alternate history in which America is colonized by

Islamic African nations and white Europeans are enslaved by wealthy African families. The novel begins in an idyllic Irish village that is soon disrupted by tribal merchants who capture men, women, and children and sell them to African enslavers. The Irish slaves must travel across the Atlantic to their bondage in the New World. The two protagonists of the novel, Kai Ali, the son of a wealthy slave owner, and Aiden O'Dere, a young boy enslaved by Kai's family, share a friendship complicated by the slave system in the new world. Barnes sets up his narrative as a direct parallel history to our own: families are torn apart by slavery, religious customs are derided by the dominant culture (in this case Christianity is the religion of the "other"), and slave owners subject their slaves to varying degrees of physical, psychological, and sexual torture. However, even as Barnes maintains an echo of American slavery in his narrative, the world of the novel and the real history of slavery remain distinct. Barnes presents readers with an alternate timeline rather than a conflation of past and present, one of the primary components of the postmodern slave narrative.[4] As a result, rather than blurring the two histories, *Lion's Blood* maintains its status as a fantastic historical romance, depicting a world separate from our own.

Neither *The Known World* nor *Lion's Blood* signal a radical break from texts like *Flight to Canada* or *The Gilda Stories*. They do, however, suggest a shift in emphasis. The texts that form the basis of this study deconstruct narrative realism as an aesthetic and an ideological form and critique its impact on the historiography of slavery. In many ways, more recent texts by black writers are the beneficiaries of the expanded palette of historical representation created by the texts that preceded them. Both historical realism and fantastic literature have become viable and revitalized modes of re-examining the history of slavery. The fact that African American writers continue to examine slavery through a diversity of forms and narrative strategies reinforces the basic belief that we can understand our present and anticipate our future only through a thorough interrogation of our past. The lasting effect of postmodern discourse on the black writer is its acknowledgement that reconstructions of the past are always contextual and always serve an ideological end. As different as *The Known World* and *Lion's Blood* are from the more radical genre crossing and deconstructive aspects of the postmodern slave narrative, they continue the tradition started by the original slave narratives themselves. They assert the need to revisit slavery through the narrative act and to destabilize our knowledge of this history.

Perhaps it is best to end by returning to the moment in *Flight to Canada* when Raven Quickskill asserts that his poem "Flight to Canada" is "a reading more than a writing" (5). Every writer of the postmodern slave narrative produces a reading of the culture that produced American slavery and maintained its legacy. What these texts remind us of is that, as readers, we perpetually make a decision as to where we place narrative authority. Reading becomes a form of writing history. In the end, this emphasis on the act of reading and interpretation as an active, ideological choice reinforces the political dimensions of postmodern aesthetics often obscured by its more abstract, theoretical claims. As such, African American approaches to postmodernism, particularly in the form of the postmodern slave narrative, rather than representing a marginalized response to the discourse at large, complicates it from within.

Introduction

1. As Robert Elliot Fox defines it, African American postmodernism addresses the black experience through the intersection of three cultural formations: the African slave trade and middle passage, the black desire for pan-African unity, and the circular view of time that connects the past, present, and future (8). I would agree that the postmodern slave narrative corresponds with at least two of Fox's definitions of African American postmodernism: its treatment of the slave experience and its orientation toward time. The postmodern slave narrative asserts the need to address the history of slavery not only because of its impact on the past but also because of its legacy in the present and future. However, Fox argues, unlike white postmodernism, African American postmodernism "puts the black back into the total historical view" and has "a strong, ethical basis rooted in the demand for, the need for, justice" (8). See *Conscientious Sorcerers: The Black Postmodernist Fiction of LeRoi Jones/Amiri Baraka, Ishmael Reed, and Samuel R. Delany* (New York: Greenwood Press, 1987).

2. It is important to note that, as a complex and varied discourse itself, postmodern theories range from those that emphasize the cultural and political vacuity of postmodern aesthetics (Baudrillard), to those that emphasize the liberating possibilities of destabilizing the totalizing narratives of Western thought (Lyotard), to those that analyze the effects of late capitalism on the postmodern condition (Jameson). Far from ignoring or rejecting the political aspects of contemporary culture, postmodern theory problematizes models of resistance based on essentialist conceptions of history, identity, and community.

3. See Ashraf Rushdy's *Neo-slave Narratives: Studies in the Social Logic of a Literary Form* (New York: Oxford University Press, 2000). According to Rushdy, neo–slave narratives comment on the cultural politics of the late sixties and recall "a historical moment in literary history when American intellectuals debated the political significance of representing the slave's voice in the work of fiction" (17). The conjunction of the Black Power movement and the publication of William Styron's *Confessions of Nat Turner* forms, for Rushdy, the moment of origin for narratives that revisit the slave narrative form.

4. Morrison has stated that her goal as a black woman writer was to gain access to the interior lives of slaves that had been obscured both by official history and by the slave narratives themselves. In order to accomplish this, Morrison felt her writing should move behind the official historical record: "Moving that veil aside requires, therefore, certain things. First of all, I must trust my own recollections. I must also depend on the recollections of others. Thus memory weighs heavily in what I write, in how I begin and in what I find to be significant. . . . But memories and recollections won't give me total access to the unwritten interior life of these people. Only the act of imagination can help me" (302). See Morrison's "The Site of Memory," in *Out There: Marginalization and Contemporary Cultures*, ed. Russell Ferguson et al., 299–305 (Cambridge: Massachusetts Institute of Technology Press, 1990).

5. Carby explores this third aspect in detail in her essay "Ideologies of Black Folk: The Historical Novel of Slavery," in *Slavery and the Literary Imagination*, ed. Deborah McDowell and Arnold Rampersad (Baltimore: Johns Hopkins University Press, 1989).

6. In his survey of the African American novel and its tradition, Bernard Bell argues that the slave narrative, along with the sentimental romance, provided "the structure and the movement" of these early novels. Many of the early novels contained one or several elements found in the two literary forms. "Family and lovers are separated and reunited; anecdotes about the evils of slavery and race prejudice are sensationally cataloged; tales of seduction of octoroons are sentimentally related; and the villain receives his just retribution while the hero marries the heroine and lives happily ever after" (55). See *The Afro-American Novel and Its Tradition* (Amherst: University of Massachusetts Press, 1987).

7. There have been numerous accounts of postmodernism that trace its trajectory from the social and cultural revolutions of the late 1960s through the neoconservative politics of the eighties. These accounts also define the general precepts of postmodernism through an analysis of its major theorists (Jean-François Lyotard, Jean Baudrillard, Fredric Jameson, among others) and discuss postmodernism's relationship to modernism. See Andreas Huyssen, *After the Great Divide: Modernism, Mass Culture, Postmodernism* (Bloomington: Indiana University Press, 1986); Steven Best and Douglass Kellner, *Postmodern Theory* (New York: Guilford Press, 1991); Linda Hutcheon, *The Politics of Postmodernism* (New York: Routledge, 1989) and *A Poetics of Postmodernism: History, Theory, Fiction* (New York: Routledge, 1988). John McGowan places postmodernism in the contexts of the Western philosophies of Kant, Hegel, Marx, and Nietzsche in *Postmodernism and Its Critics* (Ithaca: Cornell University Press, 1991). Cornel West defines postmodernism as an ideology of difference and places it in a historical context in his essay "The New Cultural Politics of Difference," in *Keeping Faith: Philosophy and Race in America* (New York: Routledge, 1993).

8. Lawrence Hogue characterizes this stance as a premodern conception of black identity and the black community. Such a conception relies on a belief "that racial communities have been isolated, that they are autonomous, homogeneous, integrated, and essentially authentic" (3). See *Race, Modernity, Postmodernity: A Look at the History and the Literatures of People of Color since the 1960s* (Albany: State University of New York Press, 1996).

9. As Ashraf Rushdy argues, the rise of black nationalism also manifested itself in debate over representations of the past, particularly the history of slavery, by prioritizing the voice of the slave over the official historical record. According to Rushdy, the

Black Power movement provided the impetus for the shift in historiography in the sixties by making the state of history in the academy socially and culturally relevant (43). See *Neo-slave Narratives: Studies in the Social Logic of a Literary Form* (New York: Oxford University Press, 1999).

10. One should note that black feminist theory arose in reaction not only to the ways black nationalism of the sixties devalued the role of women in the struggle but also to the feminist movement of the seventies which prioritized gender over race and thus ignored black women's concerns. Black feminism, then, is a corrective to multiple discourses simultaneously: white feminism, black nationalism, Eurocentrism, and, in less direct terms, postmodernism.

11. Brian McHale offers nineteenth-century narratives by Walter Scott, James Fenimore Cooper, and Leo Tolstoy as well as twentieth-century texts by Dos Passos as examples of "traditional" or "classic" historical fictions. As examples of postmodernist historical fictions, McHale cites Robert Coover's *The Public Burning,* Stanley Elkin's *George Mills,* and John Fowles's *The French Lieutenant's Woman* among numerous others. See *Postmodernist Fiction* (New York: Metheun, 1987).

12. Eagleton identifies three different postmodern conceptions of history: 1) *False utopianism:* a projection of the future into the present by relishing in the "mobility of the contemporary subject or the multiplicities of social life" (64). This view rejects the need for historical reflection and posits the fragmentation of contemporary culture as inherently liberating; 2) *Idealism:* a view which relishes in the destruction of History as a concept which results in an ability to live "decenteredly" without ends, grounds, or origins; 3) *Radicalism:* a view which emphasizes that "freedom and plurality are still to be politically created, and can be achieved by struggling against the oppressive closure of History" (65). See *The Illusions of Postmodernism* (Cambridge: Blackwell, 1996).

13. White's orientation toward history demonstrates an affinity with the ideological project of African American writers of the postmodern slave narrative. He writes:

> The recommendation that [emergent or resisting social groups] view history with the kind of "objectivity," "modesty," "realism," and "social responsibility," that has characterized historical studies since their establishment as a professional discipline—can only appear as another aspect of the ideology they are indentured to oppose. They cannot effectively oppose such an ideology while only offering their own versions . . . of this "objectivity" and so forth that the established discipline claims. This opposition can be carried forward only on the basis of a conception of the historical record as being not a window through which the past "as it really was" can be apprehended but rather a wall that must be broken through if the "terror of history" is to be directly confronted and the fear it induces dispelled. (81–82)

See *The Content of the Form: Narrative Discourse and Historical Representation* (Baltimore: Johns Hopkins University Press, 1987).

Chapter One

1. Brian McHale cites the moments when John Fowles's narrator in *The French*

Lieutenant's Woman comments on the events of the text from a contemporary perspective in spite of the fact that the narrative takes place in the nineteenth century. The narrator also infuses the title character with a modern sensibility anachronistic to her time and circumstance.

2. In an interview with Jon Ewing (1977), Reed emphasizes the link between his work, multiculturalism, and African folklore. "Voodoo is the perfect metaphor for the multicultural. Voodoo comes out of the fact that all these different tribes and cultures were brought from Africa to Haiti. All their mythologies, knowledges, and herbal medicines, their folklores jelled. It's an amalgamation like this country. Voodoo also teaches that the past is present. When I say I use a Voodoo aesthetic I'm not just kidding around." Clearly, Reed's manipulation of time goes beyond strict formalism for comedic effect and functions as a means of evoking a spiritual connection across time and multiple cultures. See "The Great Tenure Battle of 1977," *Conversations with Ishmael Reed,* ed. Bruce Dick and Amritjit Singh (Jackson: University Press of Mississippi, 1995), 111–27.

3. This marks a movement away from the dominant (and dominating) culture's view of black writing as an illustration of the slaves' humanity. The slave's ability to write, Henry Louis Gates asserts in *Figures in Black,* served as a primary argument by abolitionists against slavery (18). See *Figures in Black* (New York: Oxford University Press, 1988). William Andrews, in *To Tell a Free Story,* also points out that one of the aspects of the slave narrative that made it so popular in the nineteenth century was its connection to the "revolutionary romanticism" of the era. Many liberal readers of the day "celebrated the fugitive slave as a kind of culture-hero who exemplified the American romance of the unconquerable 'individual mind' steadily advancing towards freedom and independence" (98). See *To Tell a Free Story: The First Century of Afro-American Autobiography, 1760–1865* (Urbana: University of Illinois Press, 1986). In both these views, the act of writing served as a means of projecting a romanticized self to its readership.

4. While Reed has stated that the slave narratives by Henry Bibb, Frederick Douglass, Solomon Northrup, and others are "the best examples of what it means to live free," he specifically discusses William Wells Brown's successful manipulation of the economic and commercial aspects of his life through his money-lending business. In this sense, Brown seems to represent, for Reed, the combination of artistic and economic acumen. See *Writing Is Fighting* (New York: Atheneum, 1985).

5. The narrator of the text attributes both Raven's success and his perpetual fear of re-enslavement directly to his poem: "'Flight to Canada' was the problem. It made him famous but had also tracked him down. . . . It had dogged him" (13). The connection between the artistic representation of slavery and the dogs used to track and capture escaped slaves suggests that the dangers associated with Raven's depiction of slavery and the success it brings him pose more than just an abstract threat to his freedom. It represents a violent re-enslavement of his identity.

6. Leechfield states his view of slavery when Raven questions his motives in selling pornographic pictures depicting the sexual depravities of slavery: "I sent Swille a check. Look, Quickskill, money is what makes them go. Economics. He's got the money he paid for me, and so that will satisfy him. Economics" (74).

7. Reed's parodic treatment of history may account for the fact that he is one of the few African American writers postmodern critics like McHale and Hutcheon mention

in their work. I would argue, however, that Reed's treatment of history has more in common with other postmodern slave narratives than with white postmodern texts.

8. Butler characterizes *Kindred* as a text that lies outside the genre of science fiction in her interview with Randall Kenan. She states: "*Kindred* is fantasy. I mean literally, it is fantasy. . . . With *Kindred* there is absolutely no science involved. Not even the time travel. I don't use a time machine or anything like that. Time travel is just a device for getting the character to confront where she came from" (495–96). See "An Interview with Octavia E. Butler," *Callaloo* 14 (2) (1991): 495–504.

9. Both Dana and Kevin, when he is pulled back into the past with her, initially endure life in the past with relative ease. Dana herself points out that she has placed herself outside the events of the past: "And I began to realize why Kevin and I had fitted so easily into this time. We weren't really in. We were observers watching a show. We were watching history happen around us. And we were actors. While we waited to go home, we humored the people around us by pretending to be like them. But we were poor actors. We never really got into our roles. We never forgot that we were acting" (98). While this orientation toward the past allows her to survive, it is a distance Dana cannot maintain, nor is it one that allows her to come to terms with her own past.

10. There are several instances in the novel in which Dana must endure Alice's insults. Most of these insults involve Alice's assertion that Dana betrays her own people through her relationship with Rufus and by acting white. At one point, Dana even contemplates whether she would have liked Alice under other circumstances but acknowledges their common bond in resisting Rufus (235).

Chapter Two

1. For an in-depth discussion of the connections between gothic novels and eighteenth- and nineteenth-century depictions of slavery, see Kari Winter's *Subjects of Slavery, Agents of Change: Women and Power in Gothic Novels and Slave Narratives, 1790–1865* (Athens: University of Georgia Press, 1992).

2. Although Vijay Mishra's study concerns the European gothic novel (of which the American version is a direct descendent), his study reflects more recent tendencies to view the gothic as the expression of a political subtext rather than an element of the unconscious. See *The Gothic Sublime* (Albany: State University of New York Press, 1994). Ronald Paulson's view of the European gothic as the manifestation of eighteenth-century England's anxieties over class conflict in *Representations of Revolution, 1789–1820* (New Haven: Yale University Press, 1983) serves as another example of this reading of the gothic.

3. For a discussion of the limitations of a Freudian analysis of *Beloved,* see 396–97 of Linda Krumholz's "The Ghosts of Slavery: Historical Recovery in Toni Morrison's *Beloved,*" *African American Review* 3 (26) (1992): 395–408.

4. In her essay "Toni Morrison's Ghost: The Beloved Who Is Not Beloved," Elizabeth House uses this narrative moment to develop a provocative argument for *Beloved* being a character with a history that dates back to her home in Africa. See *Studies in American Fiction* 18 (1) (Spring 1990): 17–26.

5. As Linda Krumholz points out, a fundamental concept that informs Morrison's work is the belief that "'good' and 'evil' spring from the *methods* of categorizing and

judging, of understanding and distributing knowledge" (398). As a proponent of rationalist discourse, then, schoolteacher serves as a bridge between the gothic impulse and Enlightenment thought. See "The Ghosts of Slavery."

6. In order to maintain his authority over words and meaning, schoolteacher must resort to physical abuse. When Sixo, one of the slaves on Sweet Home plantation, challenges his authority through word play and defiant logic, schoolteacher must beat him in order to demonstrate that "definitions belonged to the definer—not the defined" (190).

Chapter Three

1. My use of the term "transculturation" reflects both the violent and nonviolent aspects of cross-cultural exchange that arose out of slavery and the middle passage. Rather than a neutral term, "transculturation" emphasizes the oppressive dimensions inherent in the transportation of Africans to America as well as the less explicitly power-laden aspects of cultural influences that occur when different cultures occupy the same space.

2. Both Toni Morrison's *Beloved* and Ishmael Reed's *Flight to Canada* contain sections of first-person narratives by former slaves but the majority of their novels use third-person narrators. The only completely first-person account of slavery in the novels I've discussed occurs in Octavia Butler's *Kindred*.

3. As James Coleman argues in his reading of Johnson's *Oxherding Tale,* Johnson "want[s] to liberate the black written tradition from what he sees as the slave narrative's legacy of narrow and limiting propaganda" (634). See "Charles Johnson's Quest for Black Freedom in *Oxherding Tale,*" *African American Review* 29 (4) (1995): 631–44.

4. Johnson goes so far as to critique the ideological dimensions of the African American literary tradition as a whole: "Image control has been the aim of black fiction—and perhaps its problem—from the very beginning of black literary production" (17). See *Being and Race: Black Writing since 1970* (Bloomington: Indiana University, 1988).

5. In an interview, Johnson criticized Toni Morrison's *Beloved,* characterizing it as "the final fruit of the Black Arts Movement" (167). See Jonathan Little, "An Interview with Charles Johnson," *Contemporary Literature* 34 (2) (1993): 159–81.

6. Even as archetypes, Johnson emphasizes Andrew's and Rutherford's transcultural dimensions. Both of these characters struggle to establish their identities within the convergence of African, European, and American cultures. By focusing on this struggle, Johnson suggests that they are products not of an essential black identity but of a fundamentally transcultural subjectivity.

7. Although in many instances it is important to make a distinction between authorial voice and the external author, in this case Johnson self-consciously draws attention to himself as the authorial voice. In the two metafictional chapters, Johnson interrupts the narrative to discuss aspects of fiction that cohere with many of the issues he raises in *Being and Race: Black Writing since 1970.*

8. Characteristic of his interest in phenomenology and the work of French theorist Merleau-Ponty, Johnson states: "Language is transcendence. And so is fiction. They comport us 'other' there behind the eyes of others, into their hearts, which might make some few of us squeamish, for suddenly our subjectivity is merged with that of a

stranger" (39). See *Being and Race.*

9. Many slave narrators began their accounts with the phrase, "I was born," and attempted to documents the date and circumstances of their birth. In some instances, the slave narrator had access to this information (Henry Bibb, James W. C. Pennington), while others could only speculate on their date of birth or parentage (Frederick Douglass, John Brown, Moses Roper). It is a parodic conceit that Andrew can place the time, place, and circumstance of his *conception.*

10. Ironically, the fact that Andrew's mother is a white woman should establish Andrew's racial identity as white. In many slave states the law dictated that a slave of mixed ancestry should follow the "station" of his mother—a law meant to enable slave owners to "produce" more slaves by raping enslaved black women. However, Anna Polkinghorne refuses to acknowledge Andrew's existence, a stance with which Jonathan Polkinghorne is more than willing to comply.

11. In his essay "The Phenomenology of the Allmuseri," Ashraf Rushdy argues that in his quest for a liberating self-conception, Andrew must reject various limiting notions of individual identity—one based on the stark intellectualism of Ezekiel; another on the perverse sexual pleasures represented by Flo Hatfield; another based on a limiting definition of race, represented by his father; another on Horace Bannon's life of violent consumption. But Rushdy missteps in claiming that Andrew finally locates his identity in Reb's liberating concept of "unpositionality" (393). Rushdy asserts that, in order to achieve this way of being, Andrew must "surrender to the world of being, to be unpositioned in the way that only Reb is unpositioned. [He] must cease to see distinctions of race, gender, and ultimately of self and other" (393). Although I agree that Andrew must come to terms with and ultimately reject conceptions of subjectivity that he encounters, Andrew rejects Reb's view along with the others he sees. See "The Phenomenology of the Allmuseri: Charles Johnson and the Subject of the Narrative of Slavery," *African American Review* 26 (93) (1992): 373–94.

12. Johnson's comic use of Marx's philosophy in the text reinforces the disjuncture between textual construction and external reality. Rather than espousing a discourse of historical materialism or a critique of slavery (or capitalism for that matter), Marx states: "Everything I've vritten has been for a voman—is one way to view Socialism, no?" (87). This ironic metafictional moment allows Johnson, in his irreverence, to poke fun at Marx's philosophy and to suggest its irrelevance for the very real capitalist institution of American slavery. See *Oxherding Tale.*

Chapter Four

1. While this is certainly the case in science fiction, it is somewhat less pronounced in the case of vampire tales, particularly with the prominence of Anne Rice and her *Vampire Chronicles.* In this instance the dominance has persisted in terms of race but not in terms of gender. Recent black writers like Tananarive Due and Nalo Hopkinson have worked extensively in fantastic literature and have established a sizeable readership. In fact, Due's 1997 novel *My Soul to Keep,* which deals with a five-hundred-year-old vampire-like character who experiences nineteenth-century slaves and contemporary freedom (much like Gomez's Gilda), has achieved both critical and popular success.

2. Even with the rise of the "new wave" science fiction of the 1960s and 1970s,

which incorporated issues of race and gender into the genre, these popular genres remained both stylistically and thematically conservative.

3. In spite of being one of the most prolific African American writers of the last twenty-five years, much less critical work has been done on Samuel Delany in comparison with other, less prolific, writers.

4. This circumstance has given way, in the last decade, to an increased (and, in many ways, dominant) emphasis on popular African American cultural forms like romance fiction. In the wake of these discursive shifts, writers like Delany and Gomez continue to be marginalized by critics even as they achieved wider appeal with readers.

5. In her article "Fantasies of Absence: The Postmodern Vampire," Veronica Hollinger argues that novels like Fred Saberhagen's *The Dracula Tape* (1973) and Jody Scott's *I, Vampire* (1984) constitute a shift toward the postmodern rejection of stable categories like "good" and "evil." See "Fantasies of Absence: The Postmodern Vampire," in *Blood Read: The Vampire as Metaphor in Contemporary Culture*, ed. Joan Gordon and Veronica Hollinger (Philadelphia: University of Pennsylvania Press, 1997), 199–212. Jewelle Gomez's work certainly shares a project with these other novels and, thus, stands as part of this postmodern refashioning of the vampire tale. See "Recasting the Mythology: Writing Vampire Fiction," in *Blood Read: The Vampire as Metaphor in Contemporary Culture*, 85–92.

6. Although some vampires in the novel subscribe to a more violent (i.e., traditional) interaction with humans, Gomez establishes the symbiotic relationship between humans and vampires as the norm. The presence of the more violent vampires prevents Gomez from offering vampirism as an idealized identity. The desire to exploit and oppress exists for vampires as it does for humans.

7. It is interesting that Bernice, one of the black women at the Woodard house, feels a discomfort with Gilda not because of the rumors surrounding her but because of her lack of a personal or familial history. Bernice feels more comfortable with Bird because, even as a vampire, she maintains connections to her past.

8. Part of Delany's connection to postmodernism derives from his use of science fiction to address the history of slavery. As Brian McHale argues, science fiction is the essential component of postmodern fiction because "it is the ontological genre *par excellence* . . . and serves as a source of materials and models for postmodernist writers" (16). McHale also acknowledges the historical novel's importance in postmodern fiction but assigns it secondary importance. See *Postmodernist Fiction.*

9. It is important to note that Korga consumes only works by women writers, texts that have been obscured by the historical record but handed down to the unnamed woman by a subversive librarian.

10. Although it is unclear what is responsible for the destruction of Rhyonon (Delany offers several possible, though inconclusive, explanations), many of the characters attribute its destruction to Cultural Fugue. Others suggest that Rhyonon was destroyed by the Xlv, alien creatures about which the Web or the General Information system knows little. The role the Xlv plays in the novel is small and open-ended. One can only suspect that Delany will explain their importance further in the second novel of the diptych.

11. Delany clearly evokes the tensions of the cold war and the threat of nuclear war, thus drawing further parallels between the contemporary moment of the book's publication and the future.

12. In his use of the term "Family," Delany evokes the patriarchy of Western culture

that maintains a hierarchical and paternalistic structure in human relations. Delany's use of the term "Sygn" in this instance invokes the metaphor of the sign in the deconstructive sense; rather than occupying a stable and unified meaning, the sign is based on multiple and shifting meanings.

13. Marq describes the structure of his family on Velm in relation to the Family conception of a family: "The father-mother-son that makes up the family unit, at least as *the* Family has described it for centuries now, represents a power structure, a structure of strong powers, mediating powers, and subordinate powers. . . . In the family structure, the parents are seen to contain and enclose the children, to protect them from society. In the stream structure, the children are the connection between the parents and society. To become a parent is to immediately have your child change your relation to society" (129). The significance of children is, therefore, their link to the larger community—each identity entwined with the whole.

Conclusion

1. Lukacs goes on to argue that, with the revolution of 1848 and the defense of middle-class privilege, the populist dimensions of the historical novel were soon replaced by texts that treated the past as spectacle, thus diminishing the radical (and potentially liberating) dimensions of the historical novel.

2. In "Realism in the Balance," Lukacs writes that Expressionism, Surrealism, and Modernism "both emotionally and intellectually remain frozen in their own immediacy; they fail to pierce the surface to discover the underlying essence, i.e. the real factors that relate their experiences to the hidden forces that produce them. On the contrary, they all develop their own artistic style—more or less consciously—as a spontaneous expression of their immediate experience" (1040). In many ways, Lukacs's critique of these forms resembles post-Marxist critics like Eagleton and Jameson's critique of postmodern aesthetics.

3. Most of the main characters in the novel have contradictory attitudes toward race and slavery. Jones includes white characters who rigorously support slavery but favor the black children they have (William Robbins), Native American characters who alternately embrace and reject their cultural identity (Oden Peoples), poor whites whose status is lower than blacks in the community (Barnum Kinsey), and black characters who fail to question the social system that allows them to enslave members of their own race (Fern Elston).

4. Barnes does, however, reinforce the "realistic" dimensions of his alternate history by tracing the roots of this reversal of colonial power to the Carthaginian defeat of Rome in 196 B.C., the continued relationship between Carthage and Egypt, and the virulence of plagues throughout Europe in the Middle Ages. Barnes suggests that these crucial differences in our history would have changed the way the Western world (and consequently slavery in the New World) developed.

Andrews, William L. *To Tell a Free Story: The First Century of Afro-American Autobiography, 1760–1865.* Urbana: University of Illinois Press, 1986.

Armitt, Lucie. "Space, Time, and Female Genealogies: A Kristevan Reading of Feminist Science Fiction." In *Image and Power: Women in Fiction in the Twentieth Century,* ed. Sarah Sceats and Gail Cunningham, 51–61. London: Longman, 1996.

Baker, Houston A., Jr. *Blues Ideology and Afro-American Literature: A Vernacular Theory.* Chicago: University of Chicago Press, 1984.

Barnes, Steven. *Lion's Blood.* New York: Warner Books, 2002.

Bartter, Martha A. "The (Science-Fiction) Reader and the Quantum Paradigm: Problems in Delany's *Stars in My Pocket like Grains of Sand.*" *Science Fiction Studies* 17 (1990): 325–40.

Bell, Bernard W. *The Afro-American Novel and Its Tradition.* Amherst: University of Massachusetts Press, 1987.

Best, Stephen, and Douglas Kellner. *Postmodern Theory.* New York: Guilford Press, 1991.

Blassingame, John W. "Black Autobiographies as History and Literature." *The Black Scholar* (December 1973–January 1974): 2–9.

Bontemps, Arna. *Black Thunder.* Boston: Beacon Press, 1968.

Botting, Fred. *Gothic: The New Critical Idiom.* New York: Routledge, 1996.

Bradley, David. *The Chaneysville Incident.* New York: Harper & Row, 1981.

Bray, Mary Kay. "To See What Our Condition Is In: Trial by Language in *Stars in My Pocket like Grains of Sand.*" In *Ash of Stars: On the Writing of Samuel R. Delany,* ed. James Sallis, 17–26. Jackson: University Press of Mississippi, 1996.

Brown, William Gells. *Clotel, or, the President's Daughter: A Narrative of Slave Life in the United States.* Boston: Bedford/St. Martins, 2000.

Butler, Octavia. *Kindred.* Boston: Beacon Press, 1979.

Butterfield, Stephen. *Black Autobiography in America.* Amherst: University of Massachusetts Press, 1974.

Carby, Hazel. "Ideologies of Black Folk: The Historical Novel of Slavery." In *Slavery and the Literary Imagination,* ed. Deborah McDowell and Arnold Rampersad, 177–98. Baltimore: Johns Hopkins University Press, 1989.

Cary, Lorene. *The Price of a Child: A Novel.* New York: Knopf, 1995.

Chase-Riboud, Barbara. *Sally Hemmings.* New York: Ballantine Books, 1994.

Coleman, James. *Black Male Fiction and the Legacy of Caliban.* Lexington: University Press of Kentucky, 2001.

———. "Charles Johnson's Quest for Black Freedom in *Oxherding Tale.*" *African American Review* 29 (4) (1995): 631–44.

Collins, Patricia Hill. *Fighting Words: Black Women and the Search for Justice.* Minneapolis: University of Minnesota Press, 1998.

Crafts, Hannah. *The Bondswoman's Narrative,* ed. Henry Louis Gates Jr. New York: Warner Books, 2002.

Delany, Samuel R. "Generic Protocols: Science Fiction and Mundane." In *The Technological Imagination: Theories and Fictions,* ed. Andreas Huyssen, Teresa De Lauretis, and Kathleen Woodward, 175–93. Madison: Coda Press, 1980.

———. *Stars in My Pocket like Grains of Sand.* New York: Bantam Books, 1990.

De Lauretis, Teresa. "Signs of Wa/onder." In *The Technological Imagination: Theories and Fictions,* ed. Andreas Huyssen, Teresa De Lauretis, and Kathleen Woodward, 158–74. Madison: Coda Press, 1980.

Domini, John. "Ishmael Reed: A Conversation with John Domini." In *Conversations with Ishmael Reed,* ed. Bruce Dick and Amritjit Singh, 128–43. Jackson: University Press of Mississippi, 1995.

Douglass, Frederick. *Narrative of the Life of Frederick Douglass, an American slave,* ed. Deborah McDowell. Oxford: Oxford University Press, 1999.

———. *The Heroic Slave.* In *Three Classic African-American Novels,* ed. William I. Andrews. New York: Mentor, 1990.

Dubey, Madhu. *Signs and Cities: Black Literary Postmodernism.* Chicago: University of Chicago Press, 2003.

Eagleton, Terry. *The Illusions of Postmodernism.* Cambridge: Blackwell, 1996.

Elkin, Stanley. *George Mills.* New York: Dutton, 1982.

Ewing, Jon. "The Great Tenure Battle of 1977." In *Conversations with Ishmael Reed,* ed. Bruce Dick and Amritjit Singh, 111–27. Jackson: University Press of Mississippi, 1995.

Foster, Frances Smith. *Witnessing Slavery: The Development of Ante-bellum Slave Narratives.* Westport: Greenwood Press, 1979.

Fowles, John. *The French Lieutenant's Woman.* Boston: Little Brown, 1969.

Fox, Robert Elliot. *Conscientious Sorcerers: The Black Postmodernist Fiction of LeRoi Jones/Amiri Baraka, Ishmael Reed, and Samuel R. Delany.* New York: Greenwood Press, 1987.

Freud, Sigmund. "The Uncanny." In *The Norton Anthology of Theory and Criticism,* ed. Vincent B. Leitch et al., 929–52. New York: Norton, 2001.

Gates, Henry Louis, Jr. *Figures in Black: Words, Signs, and the "Racial" Self.* New York: Oxford University Press, 1987.

Gilroy, Paul. *The Black Atlantic: Modernity and Double Consciousness.* Cambridge: Harvard University Press, 1993.

Gomez, Jewelle. *The Gilda Stories.* Ithaca: Firebrand Books, 1991.

———. "Recasting the Mythology: Writing Vampire Fiction." In *Blood Read: The Vampire as Metaphor in Contemporary Culture,* ed. Joan Gordon and Veronica Hollinger, 85–92. Philadelphia: University of Pennsylvania Press, 1997.

Govan, Sandra Y. "Homage to Tradition: Octavia Butler Renovates the Historical Novel." *MELUS* 13 (1–2) (1986): 79–96.

Harper, Frances E. W. *Iola LeRoy, or Shadows Uplifted.* New York: Oxford University Press, 1988.

Harper, Phillip Brian. *Framing the Margins: The Social Logic of Postmodern Culture.* New York: Oxford University Press, 1994.

Harris, Norman. "The Gods Must Be Crazy: Flight to Canada as Political History." *Modern Fiction Studies* 34 (Spring 1988): 111–23.

Henderson, Mae G. "Speaking in Tongues: Dialogics, Dialectics, and the Black Woman Writer's Literary Tradition." In *Feminists Theorize the Political*, ed. Judith Butler and Joan W. Scott, 144–66. New York: Routledge, 1992.

———. "Toni Morrison's *Beloved:* Re-membering the Body As Historical Text." In *Comparative American Identities: Race, Sex, and Nationality in the Modern Text*, ed. Hortense Spillers, 62–86. New York: Routledge, 1991.

Hogue, W. Lawrence. *Race, Modernity, Postmodernity: A Look at the History and the Literatures of People of Color since the 1960s.* Albany: State University of New York Press, 1996.

Hollinger, Veronica. "Fantasies of Absence: The Postmodern Vampire." In *Blood Read: The Vampire as Metaphor in Contemporary Culture*, ed. Joan Gordon and Veronica Hollinger, 199–212. Philadelphia: University of Pennsylvania Press, 1997.

Holloway, Karla. "Beloved: A Spiritual." In *Toni Morrison's* Beloved: *A Casebook*, ed. William Andrews and Nellie Y. McKay, 67–78. New York: Oxford University Press, 1999.

———. *Moorings and Metaphors: Figures of Culture and Gender in Black Women's Literature.* New Brunswick: Rutgers University Press, 1992.

House, Elizabeth. "Toni Morrison's Ghost: The Beloved Who Is Not Beloved." *Studies in American Fiction* 18 (1) (Spring 1990): 17–26.

Hutcheon, Linda. *A Poetics of Postmodernism: History, Theory, Fiction.* New York: Routledge, 1988.

———. *The Politics of Postmodernism.* New York: Routledge, 1989.

Huyssen, Andreas. *After the Great Divide: Modernism, Mass Culture, Postmodernism.* Bloomington: Indiana University Press, 1986.

Jameson, Fredric. *The Political Unconscious: Narrative as a Socially Symbolic Act.* Ithaca: Cornell University Press, 1981.

———. *Postmodernism, or the Cultural Logic of Late Capitalism.* Durham: Duke University Press, 1991.

Johnson, Charles. *Being and Race: Black Writing since 1970.* Bloomington: Indiana University Press, 1988.

———. *Middle Passage.* New York: Atheneum, 1990.

———. *Oxherding Tale.* New York: Grove Press, 1982.

———. "Philosophy and Black Fiction." *Obsidian* 6 (1–2) (1980): 55–61.

Jones, Edward P. *The Known World.* New York: HarperCollins, 2003.

Jones, Gayl. *Corregidora.* New York: Random House, 1975.

Jones, Miriam. "*The Gilda Stories:* Revealing the Monsters at the Margins." In *Blood Read: The Vampire as Metaphor in Contemporary Culture*, ed. Joan Gordon and Veronica Hollinger, 151–67. Philadelphia: University of Pennsylvania Press, 1997.

Kenan, Randall. "An Interview with Octavia E. Butler." *Callaloo* 14 (2) (1991): 495–504.

Kristeva, Julia. *Powers of Horror: An Essay in Abjection.* New York: Columbia University Press, 1982.

Krumholz, Linda. "The Ghosts of Slavery: Historical Recovery in Toni Morrison's *Beloved*." *African American Review* 3 (26) (1992): 395–408.

Little, Jonathan. "Charles Johnson's Revolutionary *Oxherding Tale*." *Studies in American Fiction* 2 (19) (1991): 141–51.

———. "An Interview with Charles Johnson." *Contemporary Literature* 34 (2) (1993): 159–81.

Lukacs, Georg. *The Historical Novel*. Trans. Hannah and Stanley Mitchell. Lincoln: University of Nebraska Press, 1983.

———. "Realism in the Balance." In *The Norton Anthology of Theory and Criticism*, ed. Vincent B. Leitch et al., 1033–58. New York: Norton, 2001.

McGowan, John. *Postmodernism and Its Critics*. Ithaca: Cornell University Press, 1991.

McHale, Brian. *Postmodernist Fiction*. New York: Metheun, 1987.

Mishra, Vijay. *The Gothic Sublime*. Albany: State University of New York Press, 1994.

Mitchell, Margaret. *Gone with the Wind*. New York: Macmillan, 1936.

Morrison, Toni. *Beloved*. New York: Knopf, 1987.

———. *Playing in the Dark: Whiteness and the Literary Imagination*. New York: Vintage, 1992.

———. "The Site of Memory." In *Out There: Marginalization and Contemporary Cultures*, ed. Russell Ferguson et al., 299–305. Cambridge: Massachusetts Institute of Technology Press, 1990.

———. "Unspeakable Unspoken: The Afro-American Presence in American Literature." *Michigan Quarterly Review* 23 (1989): 1–34.

Paulson, Ronald. *Representations of Revolution, 1789–1820*. New Haven: Yale University Press, 1983.

Perez-Torres, Rafael. "Between Presence and Absence: *Beloved*, Postmodernism and Blackness." In *Toni Morrison's* Beloved: *A Casebook*, ed. William Andrews and Nellie Y. Mckay, 179–202. New York: Oxford University Press, 1999.

Pyncheon, Thomas. *Gravity's Rainbow*. New York: Viking Press, 1973.

Reed, Ishmael. *Flight to Canada*. New York: Atheneum, 1976.

———. *Writing Is Fighting*. New York: Atheneum, 1985.

Rice, Ann. *Interview with the Vampire*. New York: Ballantine Books, 1977.

Rigney, Barbara Hill. "'A Story to Pass On': Ghosts and the Significance of History in Toni Morrison's *Beloved*." In *Haunting the House of Fiction: Feminist Perspectives on Ghost Stories by American Women*, ed. Lynette Carpenter and Wendy K. Kolmar, 229–35. Knoxville: University of Tennessee Press, 1991.

Rushdy, Ashraf H. A. "Daughters Signifyin(g) History: The Example of Toni Morrison's *Beloved*." *American Literature: A Journal of Literary History, Criticism, and Bibliography* 64 (3) (1992): 567–97.

———. "Families of Orphans: Relation and Disrelation in Octavia Butler's *Kindred*." *College English* 55 (2) (1993): 135–57.

———. *Neo-slave Narratives: Studies in the Social Logic of a Literary Form*. New York: Oxford University Press, 1999.

———. "The Phenomenology of the Allmuseri: Charles Johnson and the Subject of the Narrative of Slavery." *African American Review* 26 (3) (1992): 373–94.

Rushdy, Salman. *Midnight's Children*. New York: Knopf, 1981.

Samuelson, David M. "Necessary Constraints: Samuel R. Delany on Science Fiction." In *Ash of Stars: On the Writing of Samuel R. Delany*, ed. James Sallis, 109–27. Jackson:

University Press of Mississippi, 1996.

Schmudde, Carol. "The Haunting of 124." *African American Review* 26 (3) (1992): 409–16.

Smith, Allan Lloyd. "Postmodernism/Gothicism." In *Modern Gothic: A Reader,* ed. Victor Sage and Allan Lloyd Smith. Manchester, 6–19. University of Manchester Press, 1996.

Spivak, Gayatri Chakravorty. "Subaltern Studies: Deconstructing Historiography." In *The Spivak Reader,* ed. Donna Landry and Gerald Maclean, 203–36. New York: Routledge, 1985.

Stepto, Robert B. *From Behind the Veil: A Study of Afro-American Narrative.* Chicago: University of Illinois Press, 1979.

Sterne, Laurence. *The Life and Opinions of Tristram Shandy.* New York: Oxford University Press, 1983.

Stoker, Bram. *Dracula.* New York: Oxford University Press, 1966.

Tademy, Lorene. *Cane River.* New York: Warner Books, 2001.

Walker, Margaret. *Jubilee.* Boston: Houghton Mifflin, 1966.

Walsh, Richard. "'A Man's Story Is His Gris-Gris': Cultural Slavery, Literary Emancipation, and Ishmael Reed's *Flight to Canada.*" *Journal of American Studies* 27 (1) (1993): 57–71.

Webb, Frank. *The Garies and Their Friends.* Baltimore: Johns Hopkins University Press, 1997.

Weixlmann, Joe. "African American Deconstruction of the Novel in the Work of Ishmael Reed and Clarence Major." *MELUS* 17 (4) (1991–1992): 57–79.

West, Cornel. *Keeping Faith: Philosophy and Race in America.* New York: Routledge, 1993.

White, Hayden. *The Content of the Form: Narrative Discourse and Historical Representation.* Baltimore: Johns Hopkins University Press, 1987.

Williams, Sherley Anne. *Dessa Rose.* New York: Morrow, 1986.

Wilson, Harriet E. *Our Nig, or, Sketches from the life of a free Black, in a two-story white house, north, showing that slavery's shadows fall even there.* New York: Vintage, 1983.

Winter, Kari. *Subjects of Slavery, Agents of Change: Women and Power in Gothic Novels and Slave Narratives, 1790–1865.* Athens: University of Georgia Press, 1992.